TEACHER'S PET PUBLICATIONS

PUZZLE PACK
for
The Great Gatsby

based on the book by
F. Scott Fitzgerald

Written by
William T. Collins

© 2005 Teacher's Pet Publications
All Rights Reserved

The materials in this packet are copyrighted
by Teacher's Pet Publications, Inc.

These pages may be duplicated by the purchaser
for use in the purchaser's own classroom.

Copying any of these materials and distributing them
for any other purpose is a violation of the copyright laws.

© 2005 Teacher's Pet Publications, Inc.
www.tpet.com

INTRODUCTION
If you already own the LitPlan for this title, this Puzzle Pack will refresh your Unit Resource Materials and Vocabulary Resource Materials sections plus give you additional materials you can substitute into the tests. If you do not already have a complete LitPlan, these pages will give you some supplemental materials to use with your own plan. There are two main groups of materials: one set for unit words (such as characters' names, symbols, places, etc.) and one set for vocabulary words associated with the book.

WORD LIST
There is a word list for both the unit words and the vocabulary words. These lists show you which words are being used in the materials and the clues or definitions being used for those words. You may want to give students a word list with clues/definitions to help them, or you may want students to only have a word list (without clues/definitions) if you want them to work a little harder. Both are available for duplication. The word lists can also be your "calling key" for the bingo games.

FILL IN THE BLANK AND MATCHING
There are 4 each of the fill in the blank and matching worksheets for both the unit and vocabulary words. These pages can be used either as extra worksheets for students or as objective parts of a unit test. They can be done individually if students need extra help or as a whole class activity to review the material covered.

MAGIC SQUARES
The magic squares not only reinforce the material covered but also work on reasoning and math skills. Many teachers have told us that their students really enjoy doing these!

WORD SEARCH PUZZLES
The word search words go in all directions, as indicated on your answer keys. Two of the word search puzzles have the clues listed rather than the words. This makes the puzzle a little more difficult, but it reinforces the material better. Two word search puzzles have words only for students who find the clue puzzles too difficult.

CROSSWORD PUZZLES
Both unit and vocabulary word sections have 4 crossword puzzles.

BINGO CARDS
There are 32 individual bingo cards for the unit words and 32 individual bingo cards for the vocabulary words. You can use your word list as a "call list," calling the words at random and marking them off of your list as you go, or you could use the flash cards by cutting them apart and drawing the words at random from a hat (or box or whatever). To make a better review, you might ask for the definition and spelling of each word as you call it out–or you could call out the definitions and have students tell you the words they need to look for on the puzzle.

JUGGLE LETTERS
The vocabulary juggle letter game is intended to help students learn the spellings of the words. One sheet has the definitions listed on it as an extra help for students who need it or to reinforce the definitions if you choose to do so.

FLASH CARDS
We've included a set of vocabulary flash cards you can duplicate, cut, and fold for your students. Some teachers make a few sets for general use by the class; others make a set for each student. Some teachers duplicate them for each student and have the students cut & fold their own. You can cut out just the words and put them in a hat, have each student pick out one word and write the definition and a sentence for that word. Students then swap words and papers, with the next student adding a sentence of his own under the last one. You can have students swap as many times as you like. Each time the student will read the sentences written prior to his own and then add a sentence. You can cut out the words and definitions separately and play "I Have; Who Has?" Each student in the room draws a word and definition. The first student says, "I have (the name of the word). Who has the definition?" The student with the definition reads it then says, "I have (the name of the vocabulary word she has). Who has the definition?" The round continues until all words and definitions have been given.

The Great Gatsby Word List

No.	Word	Clue/Definition
1.	ADVERTISEMENT	You resemble the _____ of the man.
2.	APARTMENT	It was at 158th Street
3.	ASHES	Valley of _____; industrial zone
4.	BOATS	So we beat on, _____ against the current ....
5.	CAR	Daisy runs into Myrtle with Gatsby's
6.	CARELESS	Daisy and Tom are _____ people
7.	CARRAWAY	Nick's last name
8.	CATHERINE	Myrtle's sister
9.	CODY	Showed Gatsby how to live in the rich man's world
10.	COUSIN	Nick's relationship to Daisy
11.	DAISY	Gatsby loves her
12.	DOG	What Mrs. Wilson bought while out with Tom and Nick
13.	EGG	East or West _____
14.	EYES	_____ of Dr. T.J. Eckleburg
15.	FITZGERALD	Author
16.	FUNERAL	Few people attended Gatsby's
17.	GATSBY	Tries to impress and rekindle a relationship with Daisy
18.	GEORGE	Myrtle's husband
19.	GREEN	Color of the light on the dock
20.	HENRY	Mr. Gatz; Gatsby's father
21.	HULKING	Tom hates that word - even in kidding
22.	INVITE	Ask to come to a party
23.	JAMES	Gatsby's real name
24.	JORDAN	Miss Baker; Daisy's friend
25.	KILPSPRINGER	The boarder
26.	LEAVE	Gatsby wants Daisy to _____ Tom
27.	LUNCHEON	Gatsby had Jordan discuss this matter with Nick
28.	MANSION	It took Gatsby three years to make the money to buy this
29.	MIDWEST	Home area of the narrator
30.	MONEY	Her voice is full of _____
31.	MYRTLE	Tom's mistress
32.	ND	Initials of Gatsby's home state
33.	NICK	Narrator; Gatsby's neighbor
34.	NOSE	Tom broke Myrtle's
35.	OWLEYES	Nick met him in the library; he went to Gatsby's funeral
36.	OXFORD	Gatsby told Nick he was educated there
37.	PAMMY	Daisy's little girl
38.	PARTIES	Gatsby throws grand ones for entertainment
39.	ROOM	Wilson locked Myrtle in her _____
40.	SCHEDULE	It was in the Hopalong Casssidy book
41.	TOM	Daisy's husband
42.	TOWN	Everything's so confused, let's all go to _____
43.	WOLFSHEIM	Business associate of Gatsby

The Great Gatsby Fill In The Blank 1

1. Narrator; Gatsby's neighbor
2. Gatsby told Nick he was educated there
3. Her voice is full of _____
4. Daisy runs into Myrtle with Gatsby's
5. Initials of Gatsby's home state
6. It was at 158th Street
7. Tries to impress and rekindle a relationship with Daisy
8. Gatsby wants Daisy to _____ Tom
9. Home area of the narrator
10. What Mrs. Wilson bought while out with Tom and Nick
11. Gatsby had Jordan discuss this matter with Nick
12. East or West _____
13. Mr. Gatz; Gatsby's father
14. Business associate of Gatsby
15. Gatsby's real name
16. Myrtle's husband
17. Daisy and Tom are _____ people
18. Ask to come to a party
19. Few people attended Gatsby's
20. Color of the light on the dock

The Great Gatsby Fill In The Blank 1 Answer Key

NICK	1. Narrator; Gatsby's neighbor
OXFORD	2. Gatsby told Nick he was educated there
MONEY	3. Her voice is full of _____
CAR	4. Daisy runs into Myrtle with Gatsby's
ND	5. Initials of Gatsby's home state
APARTMENT	6. It was at 158th Street
GATSBY	7. Tries to impress and rekindle a relationship with Daisy
LEAVE	8. Gatsby wants Daisy to _____ Tom
MIDWEST	9. Home area of the narrator
DOG	10. What Mrs. Wilson bought while out with Tom and Nick
LUNCHEON	11. Gatsby had Jordan discuss this matter with Nick
EGG	12. East or West _____
HENRY	13. Mr. Gatz; Gatsby's father
WOLFSHEIM	14. Business associate of Gatsby
JAMES	15. Gatsby's real name
GEORGE	16. Myrtle's husband
CARELESS	17. Daisy and Tom are _____ people
INVITE	18. Ask to come to a party
FUNERAL	19. Few people attended Gatsby's
GREEN	20. Color of the light on the dock

The Great Gatsby Fill In The Blank 2

1. _____ of Dr. T.J. Eckleburg
2. It took Gatsby three years to make the money to buy this
3. Myrtle's husband
4. Tom's mistress
5. Gatsby's real name
6. Initials of Gatsby's home state
7. Author
8. Gatsby had Jordan discuss this matter with Nick
9. Few people attended Gatsby's
10. You resemble the _____ of the man.
11. So we beat on, _____ against the current ....
12. Everything's so confused, let's all go to _____
13. Gatsby loves her
14. Mr. Gatz; Gatsby's father
15. Showed Gatsby how to live in the rich man's world
16. Valley of _____; industrial zone
17. What Mrs. Wilson bought while out with Tom and Nick
18. Tries to impress and rekindle a relationship with Daisy
19. Color of the light on the dock
20. Daisy's little girl

The Great Gatsby Fill in The Blank 2 Answer Key

EYES	1. _____ of Dr. T.J. Eckleburg
MANSION	2. It took Gatsby three years to make the money to buy this
GEORGE	3. Myrtle's husband
MYRTLE	4. Tom's mistress
JAMES	5. Gatsby's real name
ND	6. Initials of Gatsby's home state
FITZGERALD	7. Author
LUNCHEON	8. Gatsby had Jordan discuss this matter with Nick
FUNERAL	9. Few people attended Gatsby's
ADVERTISEMENT	10. You resemble the _____ of the man.
BOATS	11. So we beat on, _____ against the current ....
TOWN	12. Everything's so confused, let's all go to _____
DAISY	13. Gatsby loves her
HENRY	14. Mr. Gatz; Gatsby's father
CODY	15. Showed Gatsby how to live in the rich man's world
ASHES	16. Valley of _____; industrial zone
DOG	17. What Mrs. Wilson bought while out with Tom and Nick
GATSBY	18. Tries to impress and rekindle a relationship with Daisy
GREEN	19. Color of the light on the dock
PAMMY	20. Daisy's little girl

The Great Gatsby Fill In The Blank 3

1. Nick met him in the library; he went to Gatsby's funeral
2. It was in the Hopalong Casssidy book
3. Gatsby throws grand ones for entertainment
4. Showed Gatsby how to live in the rich man's world
5. Business associate of Gatsby
6. Nick's last name
7. Home area of the narrator
8. Daisy's husband
9. Author
10. Wilson locked Myrtle in her _____
11. Daisy runs into Myrtle with Gatsby's
12. It was at 158th Street
13. You resemble the _____ of the man.
14. Nick's relationship to Daisy
15. Tries to impress and rekindle a relationship with Daisy
16. So we beat on, _____ against the current ....
17. Tom hates that word - even in kidding
18. Tom broke Myrtle's
19. Gatsby's real name
20. Narrator; Gatsby's neighbor

The Great Gatsby Fill In The Blank 3 Answer Key

OWLEYES	1. Nick met him in the library; he went to Gatsby's funeral
SCHEDULE	2. It was in the Hopalong Casssidy book
PARTIES	3. Gatsby throws grand ones for entertainment
CODY	4. Showed Gatsby how to live in the rich man's world
WOLFSHEIM	5. Business associate of Gatsby
CARRAWAY	6. Nick's last name
MIDWEST	7. Home area of the narrator
TOM	8. Daisy's husband
FITZGERALD	9. Author
ROOM	10. Wilson locked Myrtle in her _____
CAR	11. Daisy runs into Myrtle with Gatsby's
APARTMENT	12. It was at 158th Street
ADVERTISEMENT	13. You resemble the _____ of the man.
COUSIN	14. Nick's relationship to Daisy
GATSBY	15. Tries to impress and rekindle a relationship with Daisy
BOATS	16. So we beat on, _____ against the current ....
HULKING	17. Tom hates that word - even in kidding
NOSE	18. Tom broke Myrtle's
JAMES	19. Gatsby's real name
NICK	20. Narrator; Gatsby's neighbor

The Great Gatsby Fill In The Blank 4

_____ 1. Author

_____ 2. Gatsby throws grand ones for entertainment

_____ 3. East or West _____

_____ 4. Daisy's husband

_____ 5. What Mrs. Wilson bought while out with Tom and Nick

_____ 6. Home area of the narrator

_____ 7. Gatsby had Jordan discuss this matter with Nick

_____ 8. Mr. Gatz; Gatsby's father

_____ 9. Color of the light on the dock

_____ 10. Gatsby wants Daisy to _____ Tom

_____ 11. Gatsby told Nick he was educated there

_____ 12. Nick's last name

_____ 13. Narrator; Gatsby's neighbor

_____ 14. Wilson locked Myrtle in her _____

_____ 15. It was in the Hopalong Casssidy book

_____ 16. Gatsby's real name

_____ 17. Tom's mistress

_____ 18. Myrtle's sister

_____ 19. So we beat on, _____ against the current ....

_____ 20. Few people attended Gatsby's

The Great Gatsby Fill In The Blank 4 Answer Key

FITZGERALD	1. Author
PARTIES	2. Gatsby throws grand ones for entertainment
EGG	3. East or West _____
TOM	4. Daisy's husband
DOG	5. What Mrs. Wilson bought while out with Tom and Nick
MIDWEST	6. Home area of the narrator
LUNCHEON	7. Gatsby had Jordan discuss this matter with Nick
HENRY	8. Mr. Gatz; Gatsby's father
GREEN	9. Color of the light on the dock
LEAVE	10. Gatsby wants Daisy to _____ Tom
OXFORD	11. Gatsby told Nick he was educated there
CARRAWAY	12. Nick's last name
NICK	13. Narrator; Gatsby's neighbor
ROOM	14. Wilson locked Myrtle in her _____
SCHEDULE	15. It was in the Hopalong Casssidy book
JAMES	16. Gatsby's real name
MYRTLE	17. Tom's mistress
CATHERINE	18. Myrtle's sister
BOATS	19. So we beat on, _____ against the current ....
FUNERAL	20. Few people attended Gatsby's

The Great Gatsby Matching 1

___ 1. KILPSPRINGER   A. It was in the Hopalong Casssidy book
___ 2. CARELESS   B. Daisy and Tom are _____ people
___ 3. EGG   C. Daisy runs into Myrtle with Gatsby's
___ 4. LUNCHEON   D. Gatsby loves her
___ 5. PAMMY   E. Daisy's little girl
___ 6. JAMES   F. East or West _____
___ 7. HENRY   G. Nick's last name
___ 8. ADVERTISEMENT   H. You resemble the _____ of the man.
___ 9. OXFORD   I. Author
___10. ASHES   J. The boarder
___11. ND   K. Home area of the narrator
___12. JORDAN   L. Gatsby had Jordan discuss this matter with Nick
___13. DAISY   M. Gatsby's real name
___14. HULKING   N. Valley of _____; industrial zone
___15. FITZGERALD   O. Nick's relationship to Daisy
___16. SCHEDULE   P. Myrtle's sister
___17. GATSBY   Q. Initials of Gatsby's home state
___18. COUSIN   R. Gatsby told Nick he was educated there
___19. CODY   S. Tries to impress and rekindle a relationship with Daisy
___20. CATHERINE   T. Myrtle's husband
___21. MIDWEST   U. Tom hates that word - even in kidding
___22. GEORGE   V. Showed Gatsby how to live in the rich man's world
___23. CARRAWAY   W. Miss Baker; Daisy's friend
___24. GREEN   X. Mr. Gatz; Gatsby's father
___25. CAR   Y. Color of the light on the dock

The Great Gatsby Matching 1 Answer Key

J - 1.	KILPSPRINGER	A. It was in the Hopalong Casssidy book
B - 2.	CARELESS	B. Daisy and Tom are _____ people
F - 3.	EGG	C. Daisy runs into Myrtle with Gatsby's
L - 4.	LUNCHEON	D. Gatsby loves her
E - 5.	PAMMY	E. Daisy's little girl
M - 6.	JAMES	F. East or West _____
X - 7.	HENRY	G. Nick's last name
H - 8.	ADVERTISEMENT	H. You resemble the _____ of the man.
R - 9.	OXFORD	I. Author
N - 10.	ASHES	J. The boarder
Q - 11.	ND	K. Home area of the narrator
W - 12.	JORDAN	L. Gatsby had Jordan discuss this matter with Nick
D - 13.	DAISY	M. Gatsby's real name
U - 14.	HULKING	N. Valley of _____; industrial zone
I - 15.	FITZGERALD	O. Nick's relationship to Daisy
A - 16.	SCHEDULE	P. Myrtle's sister
S - 17.	GATSBY	Q. Initials of Gatsby's home state
O - 18.	COUSIN	R. Gatsby told Nick he was educated there
V - 19.	CODY	S. Tries to impress and rekindle a relationship with Daisy
P - 20.	CATHERINE	T. Myrtle's husband
K - 21.	MIDWEST	U. Tom hates that word - even in kidding
T - 22.	GEORGE	V. Showed Gatsby how to live in the rich man's world
G - 23.	CARRAWAY	W. Miss Baker; Daisy's friend
Y - 24.	GREEN	X. Mr. Gatz; Gatsby's father
C - 25.	CAR	Y. Color of the light on the dock

The Great Gatsby Matching 2

___ 1. WOLFSHEIM   A. Wilson locked Myrtle in her _____
___ 2. DOG   B. Ask to come to a party
___ 3. GEORGE   C. Valley of _____; industrial zone
___ 4. ADVERTISEMENT   D. The boarder
___ 5. KILPSRINGER   E. Gatsby had Jordan discuss this matter with Nick
___ 6. EYES   F. Nick met him in the library; he went to Gatsby's funeral
___ 7. ND   G. Tries to impress and rekindle a relationship with Daisy
___ 8. COUSIN   H. Her voice is full of _____
___ 9. ROOM   I. It took Gatsby three years to make the money to buy this
___10. CATHERINE   J. Daisy's little girl
___11. FITZGERALD   K. Mr. Gatz; Gatsby's father
___12. ASHES   L. What Mrs. Wilson bought while out with Tom and Nick
___13. PAMMY   M. Business associate of Gatsby
___14. OWLEYES   N. Gatsby wants Daisy to _____ Tom
___15. GATSBY   O. Author
___16. LUNCHEON   P. Gatsby loves her
___17. HENRY   Q. You resemble the _____ of the man.
___18. JORDAN   R. Nick's relationship to Daisy
___19. DAISY   S. Myrtle's sister
___20. CAR   T. Daisy runs into Myrtle with Gatsby's
___21. INVITE   U. Myrtle's husband
___22. MIDWEST   V. Home area of the narrator
___23. MANSION   W. Initials of Gatsby's home state
___24. LEAVE   X. Miss Baker; Daisy's friend
___25. MONEY   Y. _____ of Dr. T.J. Eckleburg

The Great Gatsby Matching 2 Answer Key

M - 1. WOLFSHEIM	A.	Wilson locked Myrtle in her _____
L - 2. DOG	B.	Ask to come to a party
U - 3. GEORGE	C.	Valley of _____; industrial zone
Q - 4. ADVERTISEMENT	D.	The boarder
D - 5. KILPSRINGER	E.	Gatsby had Jordan discuss this matter with Nick
Y - 6. EYES	F.	Nick met him in the library; he went to Gatsby's funeral
W - 7. ND	G.	Tries to impress and rekindle a relationship with Daisy
R - 8. COUSIN	H.	Her voice is full of _____
A - 9. ROOM	I.	It took Gatsby three years to make the money to buy this
S - 10. CATHERINE	J.	Daisy's little girl
O - 11. FITZGERALD	K.	Mr. Gatz; Gatsby's father
C - 12. ASHES	L.	What Mrs. Wilson bought while out with Tom and Nick
J - 13. PAMMY	M.	Business associate of Gatsby
F - 14. OWLEYES	N.	Gatsby wants Daisy to _____ Tom
G - 15. GATSBY	O.	Author
E - 16. LUNCHEON	P.	Gatsby loves her
K - 17. HENRY	Q.	You resemble the _____ of the man.
X - 18. JORDAN	R.	Nick's relationship to Daisy
P - 19. DAISY	S.	Myrtle's sister
T - 20. CAR	T.	Daisy runs into Myrtle with Gatsby's
B - 21. INVITE	U.	Myrtle's husband
V - 22. MIDWEST	V.	Home area of the narrator
I - 23. MANSION	W.	Initials of Gatsby's home state
N - 24. LEAVE	X.	Miss Baker; Daisy's friend
H - 25. MONEY	Y.	_____ of Dr. T.J. Eckleburg

Copyrighted

The Great Gatsby Matching 3

___ 1. HENRY   A. Gatsby loves her
___ 2. MYRTLE   B. Nick's last name
___ 3. CATHERINE   C. Gatsby's real name
___ 4. ADVERTISEMENT   D. The boarder
___ 5. LUNCHEON   E. Ask to come to a party
___ 6. MANSION   F. Wilson locked Myrtle in her _____
___ 7. ASHES   G. Daisy runs into Myrtle with Gatsby's
___ 8. KILPSPRINGER   H. Color of the light on the dock
___ 9. APARTMENT   I. It was at 158th Street
___ 10. WOLFSHEIM   J. Daisy's husband
___ 11. CARRAWAY   K. It was in the Hopalong Casssidy book
___ 12. NICK   L. Myrtle's sister
___ 13. PARTIES   M. Tom's mistress
___ 14. ROOM   N. Valley of _____; industrial zone
___ 15. DAISY   O. Gatsby had Jordan discuss this matter with Nick
___ 16. CAR   P. So we beat on, _____ against the current ....
___ 17. SCHEDULE   Q. Narrator; Gatsby's neighbor
___ 18. BOATS   R. Few people attended Gatsby's
___ 19. TOWN   S. Mr. Gatz; Gatsby's father
___ 20. TOM   T. It took Gatsby three years to make the money to buy this
___ 21. INVITE   U. Business associate of Gatsby
___ 22. MIDWEST   V. You resemble the _____ of the man.
___ 23. GREEN   W. Home area of the narrator
___ 24. FUNERAL   X. Gatsby throws grand ones for entertainment
___ 25. JAMES   Y. Everything's so confused, let's all go to _____

The Great Gatsby Matching 3 Answer Key

S - 1. HENRY	A.	Gatsby loves her
M - 2. MYRTLE	B.	Nick's last name
L - 3. CATHERINE	C.	Gatsby's real name
V - 4. ADVERTISEMENT	D.	The boarder
O - 5. LUNCHEON	E.	Ask to come to a party
T - 6. MANSION	F.	Wilson locked Myrtle in her _____
N - 7. ASHES	G.	Daisy runs into Myrtle with Gatsby's
D - 8. KILPSPRINGER	H.	Color of the light on the dock
I - 9. APARTMENT	I.	It was at 158th Street
U - 10. WOLFSHEIM	J.	Daisy's husband
B - 11. CARRAWAY	K.	It was in the Hopalong Casssidy book
Q - 12. NICK	L.	Myrtle's sister
X - 13. PARTIES	M.	Tom's mistress
F - 14. ROOM	N.	Valley of _____; industrial zone
A - 15. DAISY	O.	Gatsby had Jordan discuss this matter with Nick
G - 16. CAR	P.	So we beat on, _____ against the current ....
K - 17. SCHEDULE	Q.	Narrator; Gatsby's neighbor
P - 18. BOATS	R.	Few people attended Gatsby's
Y - 19. TOWN	S.	Mr. Gatz; Gatsby's father
J - 20. TOM	T.	It took Gatsby three years to make the money to buy this
E - 21. INVITE	U.	Business associate of Gatsby
W - 22. MIDWEST	V.	You resemble the _____ of the man.
H - 23. GREEN	W.	Home area of the narrator
R - 24. FUNERAL	X.	Gatsby throws grand ones for entertainment
C - 25. JAMES	Y.	Everything's so confused, let's all go to _____

The Great Gatsby Matching 4

___ 1. WOLFSHEIM   A. Gatsby told Nick he was educated there
___ 2. DOG   B. Tom hates that word - even in kidding
___ 3. ASHES   C. Business associate of Gatsby
___ 4. TOWN   D. Gatsby's real name
___ 5. HULKING   E. Her voice is full of _____
___ 6. FUNERAL   F. Daisy's little girl
___ 7. CODY   G. What Mrs. Wilson bought while out with Tom and Nick
___ 8. CARRAWAY   H. Nick's relationship to Daisy
___ 9. GREEN   I. Showed Gatsby how to live in the rich man's world
___10. MONEY   J. Myrtle's sister
___11. GATSBY   K. Daisy and Tom are _____ people
___12. CARELESS   L. Tries to impress and rekindle a relationship with Daisy
___13. OXFORD   M. Gatsby loves her
___14. SCHEDULE   N. Color of the light on the dock
___15. FITZGERALD   O. Everything's so confused, let's all go to _____
___16. CATHERINE   P. The boarder
___17. JAMES   Q. Nick's last name
___18. OWLEYES   R. Tom broke Myrtle's
___19. DAISY   S. Myrtle's husband
___20. NOSE   T. Nick met him in the library; he went to Gatsby's funeral
___21. GEORGE   U. Few people attended Gatsby's
___22. COUSIN   V. Valley of _____; industrial zone
___23. PAMMY   W. Author
___24. LUNCHEON   X. Gatsby had Jordan discuss this matter with Nick
___25. KILPSRINGER   Y. It was in the Hopalong Casssidy book

The Great Gatsby Matching 4 Answer Key

C - 1.	WOLFSHEIM	A.	Gatsby told Nick he was educated there
G - 2.	DOG	B.	Tom hates that word - even in kidding
V - 3.	ASHES	C.	Business associate of Gatsby
O - 4.	TOWN	D.	Gatsby's real name
B - 5.	HULKING	E.	Her voice is full of _____
U - 6.	FUNERAL	F.	Daisy's little girl
I - 7.	CODY	G.	What Mrs. Wilson bought while out with Tom and Nick
Q - 8.	CARRAWAY	H.	Nick's relationship to Daisy
N - 9.	GREEN	I.	Showed Gatsby how to live in the rich man's world
E - 10.	MONEY	J.	Myrtle's sister
L - 11.	GATSBY	K.	Daisy and Tom are _____ people
K - 12.	CARELESS	L.	Tries to impress and rekindle a relationship with Daisy
A - 13.	OXFORD	M.	Gatsby loves her
Y - 14.	SCHEDULE	N.	Color of the light on the dock
W - 15.	FITZGERALD	O.	Everything's so confused, let's all go to _____
J - 16.	CATHERINE	P.	The boarder
D - 17.	JAMES	Q.	Nick's last name
T - 18.	OWLEYES	R.	Tom broke Myrtle's
M - 19.	DAISY	S.	Myrtle's husband
R - 20.	NOSE	T.	Nick met him in the library; he went to Gatsby's funeral
S - 21.	GEORGE	U.	Few people attended Gatsby's
H - 22.	COUSIN	V.	Valley of _____; industrial zone
F - 23.	PAMMY	W.	Author
X - 24.	LUNCHEON	X.	Gatsby had Jordan discuss this matter with Nick
P - 25.	KILPSPRINGER	Y.	It was in the Hopalong Casssidy book

The Great Gatsby Magic Squares 1

Match the definition with the vocabulary word. Put your answers in the magic squares below. When your answers are correct, all columns and rows will add to the same number.

A. ASHES
B. HULKING
C. CARELESS
D. APARTMENT
E. ND
F. OXFORD
G. MIDWEST
H. CODY
I. TOWN
J. KILPSRINGER
K. DAISY
L. FUNERAL
M. COUSIN
N. GREEN
O. BOATS
P. ADVERTISEMENT

1. So we beat on, _____ against the current ....
2. It was at 158th Street
3. The boarder
4. Initials of Gatsby's home state
5. Everything's so confused, let's all go to _____
6. Gatsby told Nick he was educated there
7. You resemble the _____ of the man.
8. Daisy and Tom are _____ people
9. Showed Gatsby how to live in the rich man's world
10. Gatsby loves her
11. Valley of _____; industrial zone
12. Color of the light on the dock
13. Tom hates that word - even in kidding
14. Nick's relationship to Daisy
15. Home area of the narrator
16. Few people attended Gatsby's

A=	B=	C=	D=
E=	F=	G=	H=
I=	J=	K=	L=
M=	N=	O=	P=

The Great Gatsby Magic Squares 1 Answer Key

Match the definition with the vocabulary word. Put your answers in the magic squares below. When your answers are correct, all columns and rows will add to the same number.

A. ASHES
B. HULKING
C. CARELESS
D. APARTMENT
E. ND
F. OXFORD
G. MIDWEST
H. CODY
I. TOWN
J. KILPSPRINGER
K. DAISY
L. FUNERAL
M. COUSIN
N. GREEN
O. BOATS
P. ADVERTISEMENT

1. So we beat on, _____ against the current ....
2. It was at 158th Street
3. The boarder
4. Initials of Gatsby's home state
5. Everything's so confused, let's all go to _____
6. Gatsby told Nick he was educated there
7. You resemble the _____ of the man.
8. Daisy and Tom are _____ people
9. Showed Gatsby how to live in the rich man's world
10. Gatsby loves her
11. Valley of _____; industrial zone
12. Color of the light on the dock
13. Tom hates that word - even in kidding
14. Nick's relationship to Daisy
15. Home area of the narrator
16. Few people attended Gatsby's

A=11	B=13	C=8	D=2
A=11	B=13	C=8	D=2
E=4	F=6	G=15	H=9
I=5	J=3	K=10	L=16
M=14	N=12	O=1	P=7

The Great Gatsby Magic Squares 2

Match the definition with the vocabulary word. Put your answers in the magic squares below. When your answers are correct, all columns and rows will add to the same number.

A. CODY
B. CATHERINE
C. TOM
D. ASHES
E. LUNCHEON
F. EYES
G. MIDWEST
H. SCHEDULE
I. INVITE
J. DOG
K. GREEN
L. ROOM
M. CAR
N. DAISY
O. EGG
P. FUNERAL

1. Daisy runs into Myrtle with Gatsby's
2. _____ of Dr. T.J. Eckleburg
3. It was in the Hopalong Casssidy book
4. East or West _____
5. Wilson locked Myrtle in her _____
6. Daisy's husband
7. Showed Gatsby how to live in the rich man's world
8. What Mrs. Wilson bought while out with Tom and Nick
9. Color of the light on the dock
10. Valley of _____; industrial zone
11. Myrtle's sister
12. Ask to come to a party
13. Gatsby loves her
14. Gatsby had Jordan discuss this matter with Nick
15. Home area of the narrator
16. Few people attended Gatsby's

A=	B=	C=	D=
E=	F=	G=	H=
I=	J=	K=	L=
M=	N=	O=	P=

23
Copyrighted

The Great Gatsby Magic Squares 2 Answer Key

Match the definition with the vocabulary word. Put your answers in the magic squares below. When your answers are correct, all columns and rows will add to the same number.

A. CODY	E. LUNCHEON	I. INVITE	M. CAR
B. CATHERINE	F. EYES	J. DOG	N. DAISY
C. TOM	G. MIDWEST	K. GREEN	O. EGG
D. ASHES	H. SCHEDULE	L. ROOM	P. FUNERAL

1. Daisy runs into Myrtle with Gatsby's
2. _____ of Dr. T.J. Eckleburg
3. It was in the Hopalong Casssidy book
4. East or West _____
5. Wilson locked Myrtle in her _____
6. Daisy's husband
7. Showed Gatsby how to live in the rich man's world
8. What Mrs. Wilson bought while out with Tom and Nick
9. Color of the light on the dock
10. Valley of _____; industrial zone
11. Myrtle's sister
12. Ask to come to a party
13. Gatsby loves her
14. Gatsby had Jordan discuss this matter with Nick
15. Home area of the narrator
16. Few people attended Gatsby's

A=7	B=11	C=6	D=10
E=14	F=2	G=15	H=3
I=12	J=8	K=9	L=5
M=1	N=13	O=4	P=16

The Great Gatsby Magic Squares 3

Match the definition with the vocabulary word. Put your answers in the magic squares below. When your answers are correct, all columns and rows will add to the same number.

A. TOWN	E. ROOM	I. WOLFSHEIM	M. FITZGERALD
B. GREEN	F. CARRAWAY	J. MIDWEST	N. PAMMY
C. INVITE	G. OXFORD	K. DOG	O. CATHERINE
D. TOM	H. BOATS	L. DAISY	P. APARTMENT

1. Daisy's little girl
2. Gatsby told Nick he was educated there
3. Gatsby loves her
4. Everything's so confused, let's all go to _____
5. What Mrs. Wilson bought while out with Tom and Nick
6. Color of the light on the dock
7. Author
8. So we beat on, _____ against the current ....
9. Wilson locked Myrtle in her _____
10. It was at 158th Street
11. Ask to come to a party
12. Home area of the narrator
13. Daisy's husband
14. Business associate of Gatsby
15. Nick's last name
16. Myrtle's sister

A=	B=	C=	D=
E=	F=	G=	H=
I=	J=	K=	L=
M=	N=	O=	P=

The Great Gatsby Magic Squares 3 Answer Key

Match the definition with the vocabulary word. Put your answers in the magic squares below. When your answers are correct, all columns and rows will add to the same number.

A. TOWN
B. GREEN
C. INVITE
D. TOM

E. ROOM
F. CARRAWAY
G. OXFORD
H. BOATS

I. WOLFSHEIM
J. MIDWEST
K. DOG
L. DAISY

M. FITZGERALD
N. PAMMY
O. CATHERINE
P. APARTMENT

1. Daisy's little girl
2. Gatsby told Nick he was educated there
3. Gatsby loves her
4. Everything's so confused, let's all go to _____
5. What Mrs. Wilson bought while out with Tom and Nick
6. Color of the light on the dock
7. Author
8. So we beat on, _____ against the current ....
9. Wilson locked Myrtle in her _____
10. It was at 158th Street
11. Ask to come to a party
12. Home area of the narrator
13. Daisy's husband
14. Business associate of Gatsby
15. Nick's last name
16. Myrtle's sister

A=4	B=6	C=11	D=13
E=9	F=15	G=2	H=8
I=14	J=12	K=5	L=3
M=7	N=1	O=16	P=10

The Great Gatsby Magic Squares 4

Match the definition with the vocabulary word. Put your answers in the magic squares below. When your answers are correct, all columns and rows will add to the same number.

A. CATHERINE
B. KILPSPRINGER
C. OWLEYES
D. BOATS
E. ND
F. MYRTLE
G. GATSBY
H. ASHES
I. PAMMY
J. TOWN
K. WOLFSHEIM
L. PARTIES
M. FUNERAL
N. NICK
O. LEAVE
P. DAISY

1. The boarder
2. Tries to impress and rekindle a relationship with Daisy
3. Business associate of Gatsby
4. Narrator; Gatsby's neighbor
5. Few people attended Gatsby's
6. Gatsby throws grand ones for entertainment
7. Valley of _____; industrial zone
8. Myrtle's sister
9. Gatsby loves her
10. Daisy's little girl
11. Initials of Gatsby's home state
12. So we beat on, _____ against the current ....
13. Nick met him in the library; he went to Gatsby's funeral
14. Tom's mistress
15. Everything's so confused, let's all go to _____
16. Gatsby wants Daisy to _____ Tom

A=	B=	C=	D=
E=	F=	G=	H=
I=	J=	K=	L=
M=	N=	O=	P=

The Great Gatsby Magic Squares 4 Answer Key

Match the definition with the vocabulary word. Put your answers in the magic squares below. When your answers are correct, all columns and rows will add to the same number.

A. CATHERINE	E. ND	I. PAMMY	M. FUNERAL
B. KILPSPRINGER	F. MYRTLE	J. TOWN	N. NICK
C. OWLEYES	G. GATSBY	K. WOLFSHEIM	O. LEAVE
D. BOATS	H. ASHES	L. PARTIES	P. DAISY

1. The boarder
2. Tries to impress and rekindle a relationship with Daisy
3. Business associate of Gatsby
4. Narrator; Gatsby's neighbor
5. Few people attended Gatsby's
6. Gatsby throws grand ones for entertainment
7. Valley of _____; industrial zone
8. Myrtle's sister
9. Gatsby loves her
10. Daisy's little girl
11. Initials of Gatsby's home state
12. So we beat on, _____ against the current ....
13. Nick met him in the library; he went to Gatsby's funeral
14. Tom's mistress
15. Everything's so confused, let's all go to _____
16. Gatsby wants Daisy to _____ Tom

A=8	B=1	C=13	D=12
E=11	F=14	G=2	H=7
I=10	J=15	K=3	L=6
M=5	N=4	O=16	P=9

The Great Gatsby Word Search 1

```
A D V E R T I S E M E N T Y C R N B Q J
J M G Y Q G E T N C W B P R H V D O O S
S I D M R H I Y F C J Q D A P Y Y A X P
X D D H S V N P Q K A R S M R S T T F P
T W R A N C Q F N C W T C N S T B S O Q
B E T I Y T C F B I T O H E N S I N R F
L S F R D P T O W N Z G L E A V E E D V
T T I T M R Y P E N O E E F R E W R S K
T Y T V C V H M X D R F L O S I Y S G T
W W Z K R A T Y G A P Z U N R H N E X Y
F X G V B R R R C C Q Y N R O G E E S P
R G E G A N S F L A J E C X O W E I L T
E S R P E W G X Q R E Y H L M X A K M V
Z C A H O N K B P R L C E M G D P W K Z
Y H L S I W E N G A B J O R D A N T O M
Q E D K C S L M R W X N N U M W T N B V
B D L Z O H N E V A E X W M S C S S Q D
M U V N V R N S Y Y P W Y K Q I O B B N
H L S T N U J A M E S N G G M C N D T Y
N E R M F V D M A N S I O N E L T R Y M
```

Ask to come to a party (6)
Author (10)
Business associate of Gatsby (9)
Color of the light on the dock (5)
Daisy and Tom are _____ people (8)
Daisy runs into Myrtle with Gatsby's (3)
Daisy's husband (3)
Daisy's little girl (5)
East or West _____ (3)
Everything's so confused, let's all go to _____ (4)
Few people attended Gatsby's (7)
Gatsby had Jordan discuss this matter with Nick (8)
Gatsby loves her (5)
Gatsby throws grand ones for entertainment (7)
Gatsby told Nick he was educated there (6)
Gatsby wants Daisy to _____ Tom (5)
Gatsby's real name (5)
Her voice is full of _____ (5)
Home area of the narrator (7)
Initials of Gatsby's home state (2)
It took Gatsby three years to make the money to buy this (7)
It was at 158th Street (9)

It was in the Hopalong Casssidy book (8)
Miss Baker; Daisy's friend (6)
Mr. Gatz; Gatsby's father (5)
Myrtle's husband (6)
Myrtle's sister (9)
Narrator; Gatsby's neighbor (4)
Nick met him in the library; he went to Gatsby's funeral (7)
Nick's last name (8)
Nick's relationship to Daisy (6)
Showed Gatsby how to live in the rich man's world (4)
So we beat on, _____ against the current .... (5)
Tom broke Myrtle's (4)
Tom hates that word - even in kidding (7)
Tom's mistress (6)
Tries to impress and rekindle a relationship with Daisy (6)
Valley of _____; industrial zone (5)
What Mrs. Wilson bought while out with Tom and Nick (3)
Wilson locked Myrtle in her _____ (4)
You resemble the _____ of the man. (13)
_____ of Dr. T.J. Eckleburg (4)

The Great Gatsby Word Search 1 Answer Key

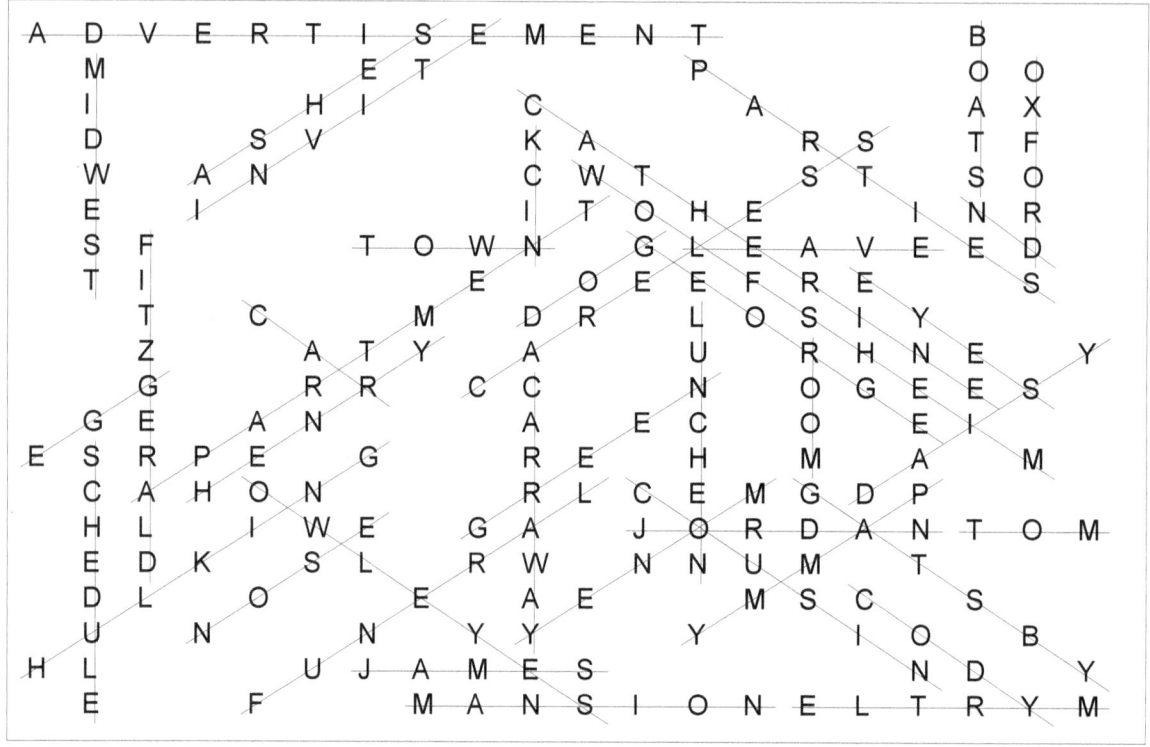

Ask to come to a party (6)
Author (10)
Business associate of Gatsby (9)
Color of the light on the dock (5)
Daisy and Tom are _____ people (8)
Daisy runs into Myrtle with Gatsby's (3)
Daisy's husband (3)
Daisy's little girl (5)
East or West _____ (3)
Everything's so confused, let's all go to
  _____ (4)
Few people attended Gatsby's (7)
Gatsby had Jordan discuss this matter with
  Nick (8)
Gatsby loves her (5)
Gatsby throws grand ones for entertainment
  (7)
Gatsby told Nick he was educated there (6)
Gatsby wants Daisy to _____ Tom (5)
Gatsby's real name (5)
Her voice is full of _____ (5)
Home area of the narrator (7)
Initials of Gatsby's home state (2)
It took Gatsby three years to make the money
  to buy this (7)
It was at 158th Street (9)

It was in the Hopalong Casssidy book (8)
Miss Baker; Daisy's friend (6)
Mr. Gatz; Gatsby's father (5)
Myrtle's husband (6)
Myrtle's sister (9)
Narrator; Gatsby's neighbor (4)
Nick met him in the library; he went to
  Gatsby's funeral (7)
Nick's last name (8)
Nick's relationship to Daisy (6)
Showed Gatsby how to live in the rich man's
  world (4)
So we beat on, _____ against the current ....
  (5)
Tom broke Myrtle's (4)
Tom hates that word - even in kidding (7)
Tom's mistress (6)
Tries to impress and rekindle a relationship
  with Daisy (6)
Valley of _____; industrial zone (5)
What Mrs. Wilson bought while out with Tom
  and Nick (3)
Wilson locked Myrtle in her _____ (4)
You resemble the _____ of the man. (13)
_____ of Dr. T.J. Eckleburg (4)

The Great Gatsby Word Search 2

```
M I W X W S M W J L P S L U N C H E O N
A O N S J O J Z M O T X V R I D J G N S
D C N V J V L K D A R J X J S J J M L K
V A A E I B J F O S C D H L U W V B G R
E R R T Y T N B S M M C A T O P A M M Y
R E J M H E E V C H Y R G N C J G F C S
T L R R D E S A X T E R M O R P R H K G
I E O X F O R D K N D I T W K L E J J B
S S T L C R P I U C G B M L W H E G N Q
E S G G A S R F N R B J C E E U N M G F
M B J W R P L M V E R D M Y C L L A A D
E G A L N M L I D B L D M E T K C N T G
N Y X Q D O Y D L A N P F S E I X S S H
T L M S W T S W R B I P L L Z N C I B T
K A P A R T M E N T M S U D O G N O Y J
C G J T V J G S Z O E D Y Y G E D N D N
A Y H W J Z G T T H E R R E T O W W R Y
R P A R T I E S S H D N I C K R M O O T
V N S I F G Y A C P E L J V S G G T O P
G N F J A M E S W H L E A V E E F S M Q
```

Ask to come to a party (6)
Author (10)
Business associate of Gatsby (9)
Color of the light on the dock (5)
Daisy and Tom are _____ people (8)
Daisy runs into Myrtle with Gatsby's (3)
Daisy's husband (3)
Daisy's little girl (5)
East or West _____ (3)
Everything's so confused, let's all go to _____ (4)
Few people attended Gatsby's (7)
Gatsby had Jordan discuss this matter with Nick (8)
Gatsby loves her (5)
Gatsby throws grand ones for entertainment (7)
Gatsby told Nick he was educated there (6)
Gatsby wants Daisy to _____ Tom (5)
Gatsby's real name (5)
Her voice is full of _____ (5)
Home area of the narrator (7)
Initials of Gatsby's home state (2)
It took Gatsby three years to make the money to buy this (7)
It was at 158th Street (9)
It was in the Hopalong Casssidy book (8)
Miss Baker; Daisy's friend (6)
Mr. Gatz; Gatsby's father (5)
Myrtle's husband (6)
Myrtle's sister (9)
Narrator; Gatsby's neighbor (4)
Nick met him in the library; he went to Gatsby's funeral (7)
Nick's last name (8)
Nick's relationship to Daisy (6)
Showed Gatsby how to live in the rich man's world (4)
So we beat on, _____ against the current .... (5)
Tom broke Myrtle's (4)
Tom hates that word - even in kidding (7)
Tom's mistress (6)
Tries to impress and rekindle a relationship with Daisy (6)
Valley of _____; industrial zone (5)
What Mrs. Wilson bought while out with Tom and Nick (3)
Wilson locked Myrtle in her _____ (4)
You resemble the _____ of the man. (13)
_____ of Dr. T.J. Eckleburg (4)

The Great Gatsby Word Search 2 Answer Key

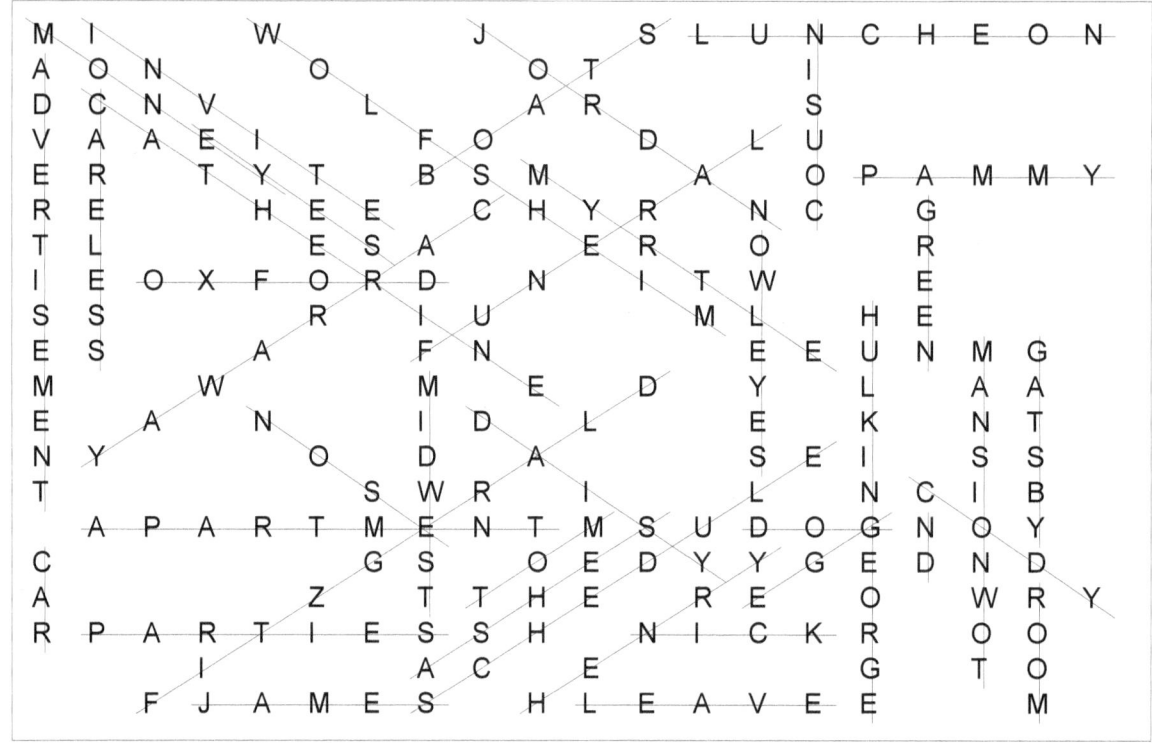

Ask to come to a party (6)
Author (10)
Business associate of Gatsby (9)
Color of the light on the dock (5)
Daisy and Tom are _____ people (8)
Daisy runs into Myrtle with Gatsby's (3)
Daisy's husband (3)
Daisy's little girl (5)
East or West _____ (3)
Everything's so confused, let's all go to _____ (4)
Few people attended Gatsby's (7)
Gatsby had Jordan discuss this matter with Nick (8)
Gatsby loves her (5)
Gatsby throws grand ones for entertainment (7)
Gatsby told Nick he was educated there (6)
Gatsby wants Daisy to _____ Tom (5)
Gatsby's real name (5)
Her voice is full of _____ (5)
Home area of the narrator (7)
Initials of Gatsby's home state (2)
It took Gatsby three years to make the money to buy this (7)
It was at 158th Street (9)

It was in the Hopalong Casssidy book (8)
Miss Baker; Daisy's friend (6)
Mr. Gatz; Gatsby's father (5)
Myrtle's husband (6)
Myrtle's sister (9)
Narrator; Gatsby's neighbor (4)
Nick met him in the library; he went to Gatsby's funeral (7)
Nick's last name (8)
Nick's relationship to Daisy (6)
Showed Gatsby how to live in the rich man's world (4)
So we beat on, _____ against the current .... (5)
Tom broke Myrtle's (4)
Tom hates that word - even in kidding (7)
Tom's mistress (6)
Tries to impress and rekindle a relationship with Daisy (6)
Valley of _____; industrial zone (5)
What Mrs. Wilson bought while out with Tom and Nick (3)
Wilson locked Myrtle in her _____ (4)
You resemble the _____ of the man. (13)
_____ of Dr. T.J. Eckleburg (4)

The Great Gatsby Word Search 3

```
I F J Z H C A R E L E S S C V C G S Q M
N M D T S U G J K P Q M Z B S L B C G F
V W W V N R L S X Z L T D L S P R H K J
I F C B Y M R K R W L B F X S N M E Q Z
T I C S H N Y C I P D X F H G K S D Y D
E T V Z N J A N R N R X X U Y C K U B N
F Z C C B R K D M S G N W N N R Z L X C
N G M Z R D D D V Y Z N P J Y E D E B F
Y E D A B A M Z K E B W X B V P R O Z P
M R W N N I Z Y F M R O S V P M A A E Y
C A R N O S E A P A R T M E N T K G L L
Y L S T D Y I A W B A S I D S B O U T P
O D Q H W Z R O E G C E N S V D N G R W
F W K S E T Z K N O O W M M E C J R Y X
M O L Y I S B I I X U D Q Q H M R E M Z
X L P E E J Q L R F S I Y E Y H E E F Q
S F S G Y G C P E O I M O N K Y G N M F
V S D F E E T S H R N N A C R R G O T Z
C H V J S B S P T D F D I N Q M O G B Z
R E C T B N T R A H R N E J T R X E P C
W I L O Z Q O I C O L H P A M M Y O F X
V M V F D D M N J Y E L R M R O L R Q Q
S L D Q Y Y C G W X A W J E M N F G T K
D B X L Y Z W E P Y V F F S Y E N E F S
L G Q S K P Q R Z N E M R T M Y N R Z P
```

ADVERTISEMENT	DOG	JAMES	NOSE
APARTMENT	EGG	JORDAN	OWLEYES
ASHES	EYES	KILPSPRINGER	OXFORD
BOATS	FITZGERALD	LEAVE	PAMMY
CAR	FUNERAL	LUNCHEON	PARTIES
CARELESS	GATSBY	MANSION	ROOM
CARRAWAY	GEORGE	MIDWEST	SCHEDULE
CATHERINE	GREEN	MONEY	TOM
CODY	HENRY	MYRTLE	TOWN
COUSIN	HULKING	ND	WOLFSHEIM
DAISY	INVITE	NICK	

The Great Gatsby Word Search 3 Answer Key

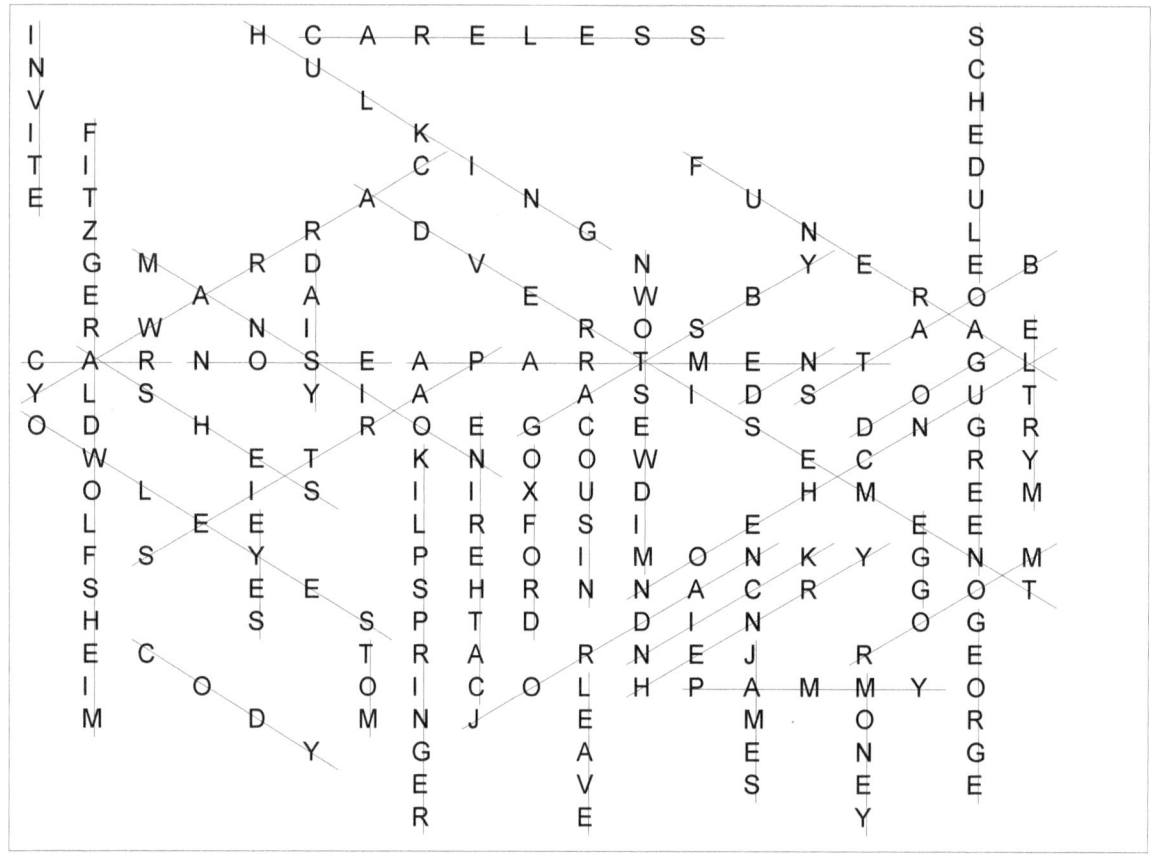

ADVERTISEMENT	DOG	JAMES	NOSE
APARTMENT	EGG	JORDAN	OWLEYES
ASHES	EYES	KILPSPRINGER	OXFORD
BOATS	FITZGERALD	LEAVE	PAMMY
CAR	FUNERAL	LUNCHEON	PARTIES
CARELESS	GATSBY	MANSION	ROOM
CARRAWAY	GEORGE	MIDWEST	SCHEDULE
CATHERINE	GREEN	MONEY	TOM
CODY	HENRY	MYRTLE	TOWN
COUSIN	HULKING	ND	WOLFSHEIM
DAISY	INVITE	NICK	

The Great Gatsby Word Search 4

```
Q B X F V W B W T W Z G M C S Y Z B R T
G V F S G P Q B V H L R T G P K Z D S V
C M F K A S C L X T Q R B K L P Z J C R
P M W F C D O Q Y V K Z J T T J Q S H L
H Y S M D W V G H K P S O Z L C T J E X
Q U M K L M R E D K A Q R C O E Q M D N
C R L E H E K Y R N R N D Y X F A M U D
A K Y K E C A E G T T M A T F S D V L S
R E G N I R P S P L I K N N O M O N E Y
S O G N Q N S Y H E E S D L R M G M N F
Y J O G K E G L H E S C E N D Z A F I P
G Y X M L N U S T Q S H E M F J Y I R B
N D T E H N F K M B M G V Y E Y B T E L
Z K R W C L O M B I R F G R C N S Z H Z
V A X H O R Z S R O D N B T O B T G T M
C W E W W A N D E M P W H L D N A E A L
T O D B Q C P G V N A I E E Y N G R C D
N H A F Y P V A I Q M N Y S Q N K A A F
M E I J U Z G S R J M V S L T Z F L R R
G N S Z X N U R S T Y I Q I T O F D R K
G R Y X T O E T Q Z M T V T O C W J A T
F Y C B C T A R F Y G E Q Z S N P N W Z
J G G H G O Z L A Y M Y N B P D K B A K
X H M M B N F Q B L L G W T H Y X G Y X
M L F Y G L W Y H W K J D J X R T N B T
```

ADVERTISEMENT	DOG	JAMES	NOSE
APARTMENT	EGG	JORDAN	OWLEYES
ASHES	EYES	KILPSPRINGER	OXFORD
BOATS	FITZGERALD	LEAVE	PAMMY
CAR	FUNERAL	LUNCHEON	PARTIES
CARELESS	GATSBY	MANSION	ROOM
CARRAWAY	GEORGE	MIDWEST	SCHEDULE
CATHERINE	GREEN	MONEY	TOM
CODY	HENRY	MYRTLE	TOWN
COUSIN	HULKING	ND	WOLFSHEIM
DAISY	INVITE	NICK	

The Great Gatsby Word Search 4 Answer Key

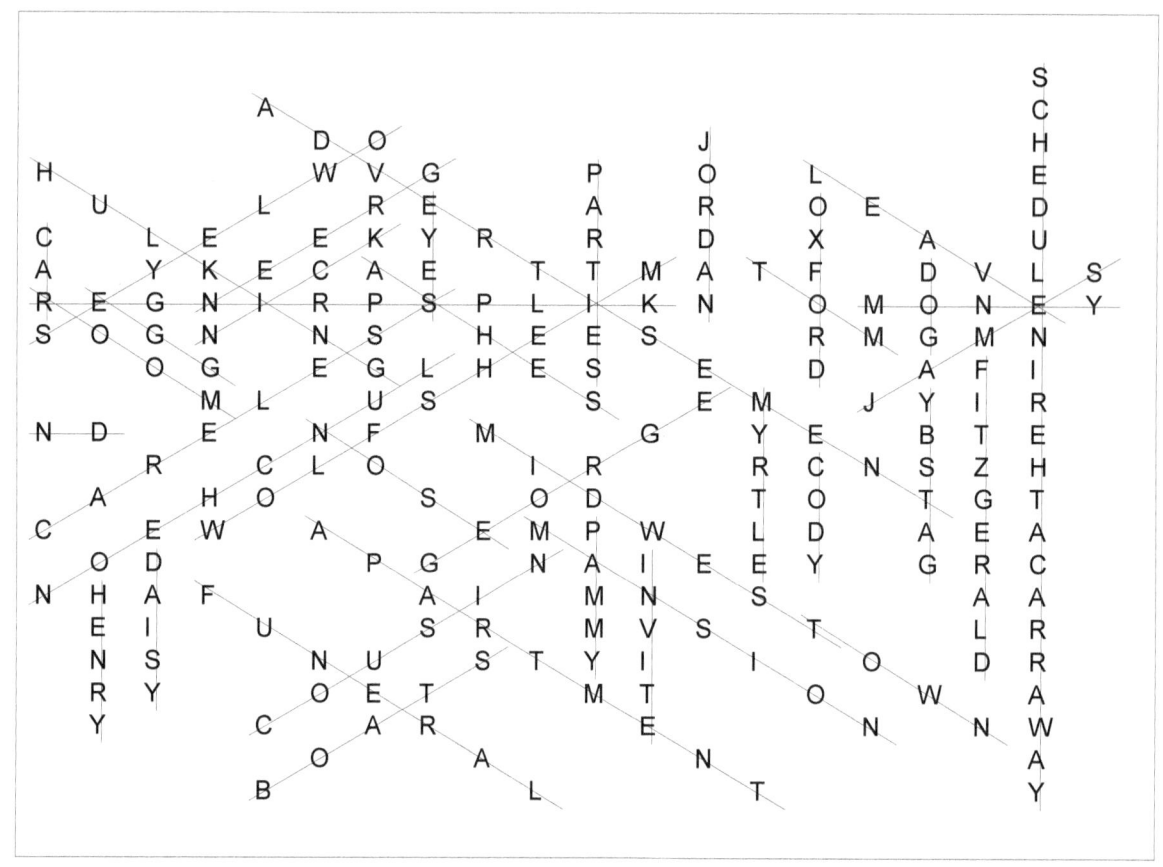

ADVERTISEMENT	DOG	JAMES	NOSE
APARTMENT	EGG	JORDAN	OWLEYES
ASHES	EYES	KILPSRINGER	OXFORD
BOATS	FITZGERALD	LEAVE	PAMMY
CAR	FUNERAL	LUNCHEON	PARTIES
CARELESS	GATSBY	MANSION	ROOM
CARRAWAY	GEORGE	MIDWEST	SCHEDULE
CATHERINE	GREEN	MONEY	TOM
CODY	HENRY	MYRTLE	TOWN
COUSIN	HULKING	ND	WOLFSHEIM
DAISY	INVITE	NICK	

The Great Gatsby Crossword 1

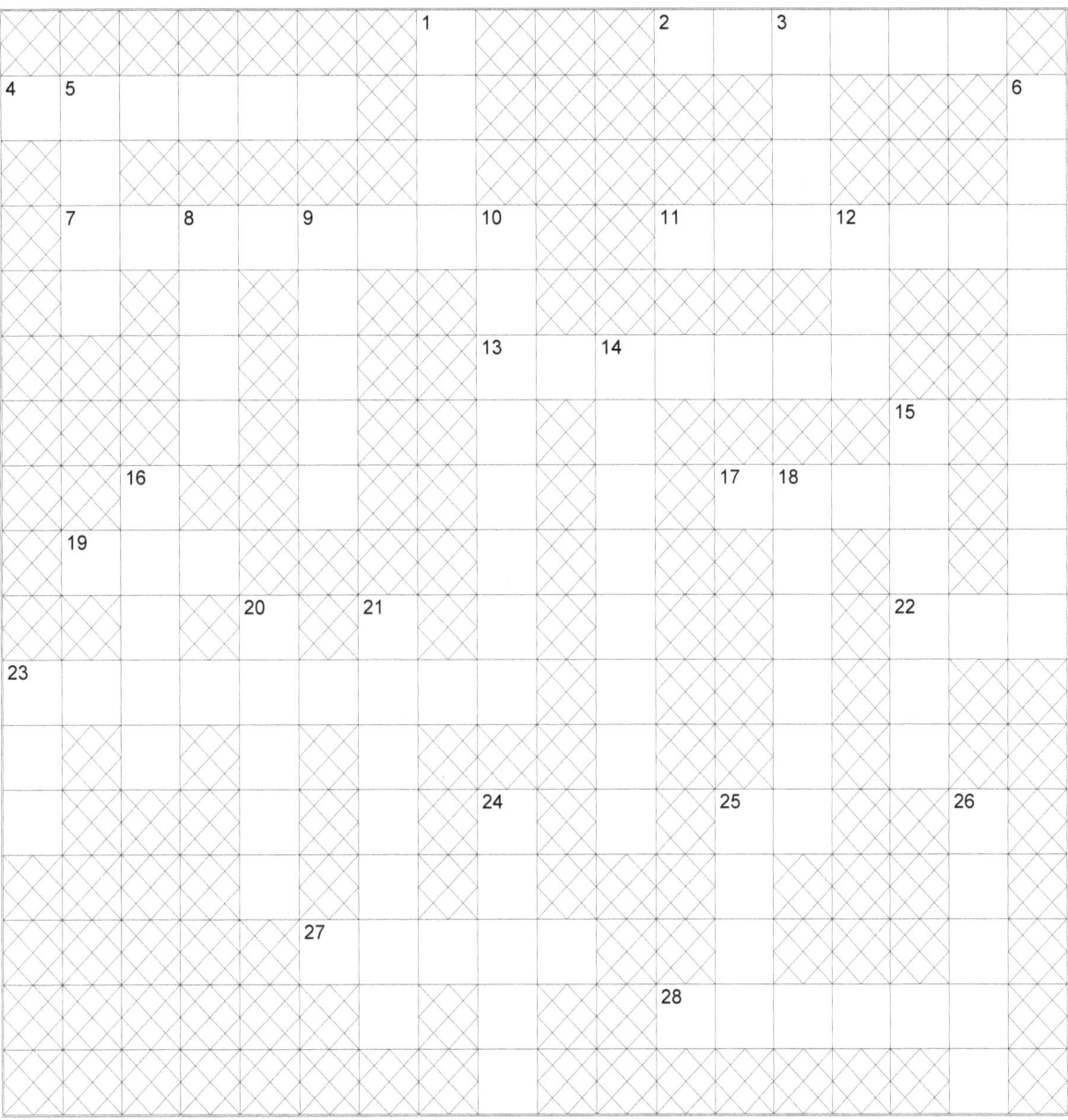

Across
2. Tries to impress and rekindle a relationship with Daisy
4. Ask to come to a party
7. Daisy and Tom are _____ people
11. Few people attended Gatsby's
13. Tom hates that word - even in kidding
17. Showed Gatsby how to live in the rich man's world
19. What Mrs. Wilson bought while out with Tom and Nick
22. Daisy's husband
23. Myrtle's sister
25. Initials of Gatsby's home state
27. Valley of _____; industrial zone
28. Myrtle's husband

Down
1. _____ of Dr. T.J. Eckleburg
3. Everything's so confused, let's all go to _____
5. Narrator; Gatsby's neighbor
6. Business associate of Gatsby
8. Wilson locked Myrtle in her _____
9. Gatsby wants Daisy to _____ Tom
10. It was in the Hopalong Casssidy book
12. East or West _____
14. Gatsby had Jordan discuss this matter with Nick
15. Tom's mistress
16. So we beat on, _____ against the current ....
18. Gatsby told Nick he was educated there
20. Mr. Gatz; Gatsby's father
21. Home area of the narrator
23. Daisy runs into Myrtle with Gatsby's
24. Color of the light on the dock
25. Tom broke Myrtle's
26. Her voice is full of _____

The Great Gatsby Crossword 1 Answer Key

						1 E		2 G	3 A	T	S	B	Y	
4 I	5 N	V	I	T	E	Y			T	O				6 W
	I					E				W				O
	7 C	8 A	R	9 E	L	10 E	S	S		11 F	U	N	12 E	R	A	L
	K	O		E		C						G		F
		O		A		13 H	14 U	L	K	I	N	G		S
		M		V		E		U					15 M	H
	16 B			E		D		N		17 C	18 O	D	Y	E
19 D	O	G				U		C		X	R			I
	A		20 H		21 M	L		H			F		22 T	O	M
23 C	A	T	H	E	R	I	N	E			O		L	
A		S		N		D		O			R		E	
R				R		24 W		25 G	R	N	D		26 M
				Y		E				O			O
				27 A	S	H	E	S		S			N
				T		E			28 G	E	O	R	G	E
						N							Y

Across
2. Tries to impress and rekindle a relationship with Daisy
4. Ask to come to a party
7. Daisy and Tom are _____ people
11. Few people attended Gatsby's
13. Tom hates that word - even in kidding
17. Showed Gatsby how to live in the rich man's world
19. What Mrs. Wilson bought while out with Tom and Nick
22. Daisy's husband
23. Myrtle's sister
25. Initials of Gatsby's home state
27. Valley of _____; industrial zone
28. Myrtle's husband

Down
1. _____ of Dr. T.J. Eckleburg
3. Everything's so confused, let's all go to _____
5. Narrator; Gatsby's neighbor
6. Business associate of Gatsby
8. Wilson locked Myrtle in her _____
9. Gatsby wants Daisy to _____ Tom
10. It was in the Hopalong Casssidy book
12. East or West _____
14. Gatsby had Jordan discuss this matter with Nick
15. Tom's mistress
16. So we beat on, _____ against the current ....
18. Gatsby told Nick he was educated there
20. Mr. Gatz; Gatsby's father
21. Home area of the narrator
23. Daisy runs into Myrtle with Gatsby's
24. Color of the light on the dock
25. Tom broke Myrtle's
26. Her voice is full of _____

The Great Gatsby Crossword 2

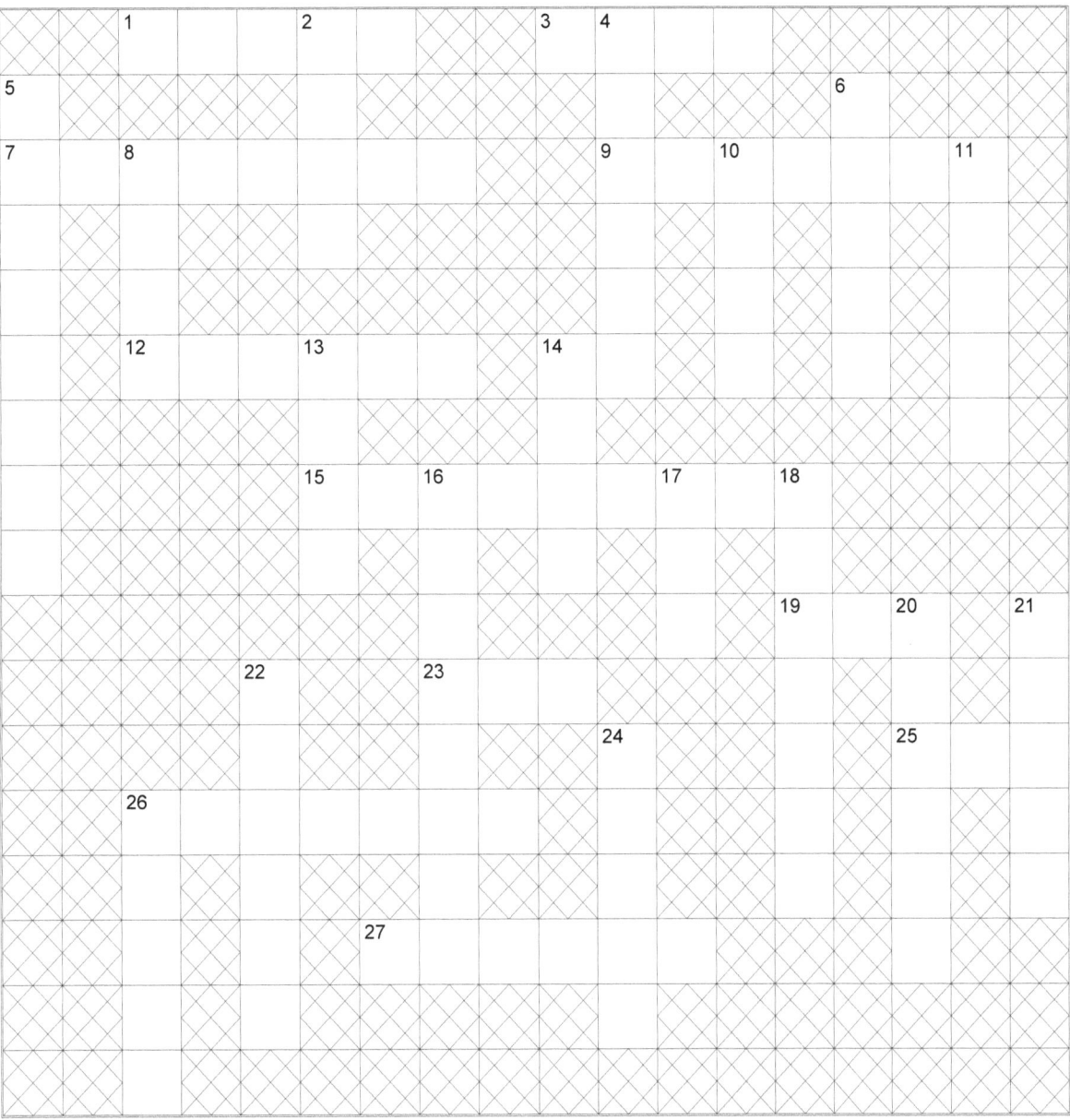

Across
1. Her voice is full of _____
3. Showed Gatsby how to live in the rich man's world
7. Daisy and Tom are _____ people
9. Few people attended Gatsby's
12. Tom's mistress
14. Initials of Gatsby's home state
15. Business associate of Gatsby
19. What Mrs. Wilson bought while out with Tom and Nick
23. Daisy runs into Myrtle with Gatsby's
25. Daisy's husband
26. Gatsby throws grand ones for entertainment
27. Ask to come to a party

Down
2. _____ of Dr. T.J. Eckleburg
4. Gatsby told Nick he was educated there
5. It was in the Hopalong Casssidy book
6. Color of the light on the dock
8. Wilson locked Myrtle in her _____
10. Narrator; Gatsby's neighbor
11. Gatsby wants Daisy to _____ Tom
13. Everything's so confused, let's all go to _____
14. Tom broke Myrtle's
16. Gatsby had Jordan discuss this matter with Nick
17. East or West _____
18. Home area of the narrator
20. Tries to impress and rekindle a relationship with Daisy
21. Gatsby's real name
22. Miss Baker; Daisy's friend
24. So we beat on, _____ against the current ....
26. Daisy's little girl

The Great Gatsby Crossword 2 Answer Key

		1 M	O	2 N	E	Y		3 C	4 O	D	Y			
5 S				Y				X					6 G	
7 C	8 A	R	E	L	E	S	S		9 F	10 U	N	E	R	11 A	L
H	R	O			S				O	I		E		L
E	O								R	C		E		A
D	12 M	Y	R	13 T	L	E		14 N	D	K		N		V
U				O				O						E
L				15 W	O	16 L	F	17 S	H	18 E	I	M	
E						N		U		E		I	
						N		E		G		19 D	O	20 G	21 J
			22 J		23 C	A	R					W		A	A
			O		H				24 B		E		25 T	O	M
		26 P	A	R	T	I	E	S		O		S		S	E
		A		D			O			A		T		B	S
		M		A		27 I	N	V	I	T	E			Y
		M		N			S			S				
		Y												

Across
1. Her voice is full of _____
3. Showed Gatsby how to live in the rich man's world
7. Daisy and Tom are _____ people
9. Few people attended Gatsby's
12. Tom's mistress
14. Initials of Gatsby's home state
15. Business associate of Gatsby
19. What Mrs. Wilson bought while out with Tom and Nick
23. Daisy runs into Myrtle with Gatsby's
25. Daisy's husband
26. Gatsby throws grand ones for entertainment
27. Ask to come to a party

Down
2. _____ of Dr. T.J. Eckleburg
4. Gatsby told Nick he was educated there
5. It was in the Hopalong Casssidy book
6. Color of the light on the dock
8. Wilson locked Myrtle in her _____
10. Narrator; Gatsby's neighbor
11. Gatsby wants Daisy to _____ Tom
13. Everything's so confused, let's all go to _____
14. Tom broke Myrtle's
16. Gatsby had Jordan discuss this matter with Nick
17. East or West _____
18. Home area of the narrator
20. Tries to impress and rekindle a relationship with Daisy
21. Gatsby's real name
22. Miss Baker; Daisy's friend
24. So we beat on, _____ against the current ....
26. Daisy's little girl

The Great Gatsby Crossword 3

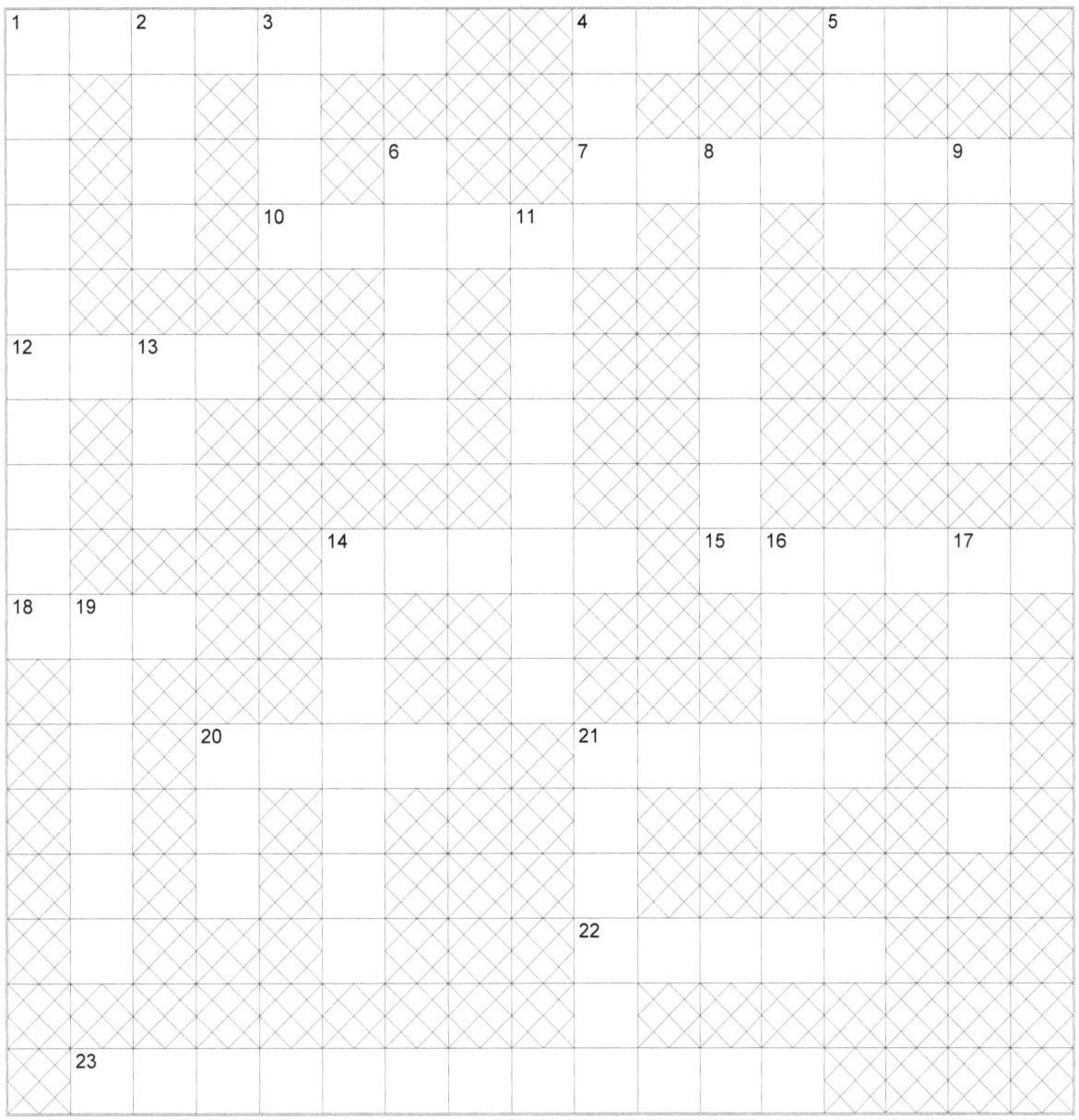

Across
1. Few people attended Gatsby's
4. Initials of Gatsby's home state
5. Daisy runs into Myrtle with Gatsby's
7. It was in the Hopalong Casssidy book
10. Tom's mistress
12. _____ of Dr. T.J. Eckleburg
14. Her voice is full of _____
15. Tries to impress and rekindle a relationship with Daisy
18. What Mrs. Wilson bought while out with Tom and Nick
20. Everything's so confused, let's all go to _____
21. Gatsby's real name
22. Gatsby loves her
23. The boarder

Down
1. Author
2. Narrator; Gatsby's neighbor
3. Wilson locked Myrtle in her _____
4. Tom broke Myrtle's
5. Showed Gatsby how to live in the rich man's world
6. Color of the light on the dock
8. Tom hates that word - even in kidding
9. Gatsby wants Daisy to _____ Tom
11. Gatsby had Jordan discuss this matter with Nick
13. East or West _____
14. Home area of the narrator
16. Valley of _____; industrial zone
17. So we beat on, _____ against the current ....
19. Gatsby told Nick he was educated there
20. Daisy's husband
21. Miss Baker; Daisy's friend

The Great Gatsby Crossword 3 Answer Key

	1 F	2 U	N	3 E	R	A	L		4 N	D			5 C	A	R	
	I		I		O				O				O			
	T		C		O		6 G		7 S	C	8 H	E	D	U	9 L	E
	Z		K		10 M	Y	R	11 T	L	E						
											U				Y		E
	G						E		U		L						A
	12 E	Y	13 E	S			E		N		K				V	
	R		G				N		C		I				E	
	A		G						H		N					
	L					14 M	O	N	E	Y	15 G	16 A	T	S	17 B	Y
18 D	19 O	G			I			O			S				O	
	X				D			N			H				A	
	F		20 T	O	W	N		21 J	A	M	E	S			T	
	O		O		E			O			S				S	
	R		M		S			R								
	D				T			22 D	A	I	S	Y				
								A								
	23 K	I	L	P	S	P	R	I	N	G	E	R				

Across
1. Few people attended Gatsby's
4. Initials of Gatsby's home state
5. Daisy runs into Myrtle with Gatsby's
7. It was in the Hopalong Casssidy book
10. Tom's mistress
12. _____ of Dr. T.J. Eckleburg
14. Her voice is full of _____
15. Tries to impress and rekindle a relationship with Daisy
18. What Mrs. Wilson bought while out with Tom and Nick
20. Everything's so confused, let's all go to _____
21. Gatsby's real name
22. Gatsby loves her
23. The boarder

Down
1. Author
2. Narrator; Gatsby's neighbor
3. Wilson locked Myrtle in her _____
4. Tom broke Myrtle's
5. Showed Gatsby how to live in the rich man's world
6. Color of the light on the dock
8. Tom hates that word - even in kidding
9. Gatsby wants Daisy to _____ Tom
11. Gatsby had Jordan discuss this matter with Nick
13. East or West _____
14. Home area of the narrator
16. Valley of _____; industrial zone
17. So we beat on, _____ against the current ....
19. Gatsby told Nick he was educated there
20. Daisy's husband
21. Miss Baker; Daisy's friend

The Great Gatsby Crossword 4

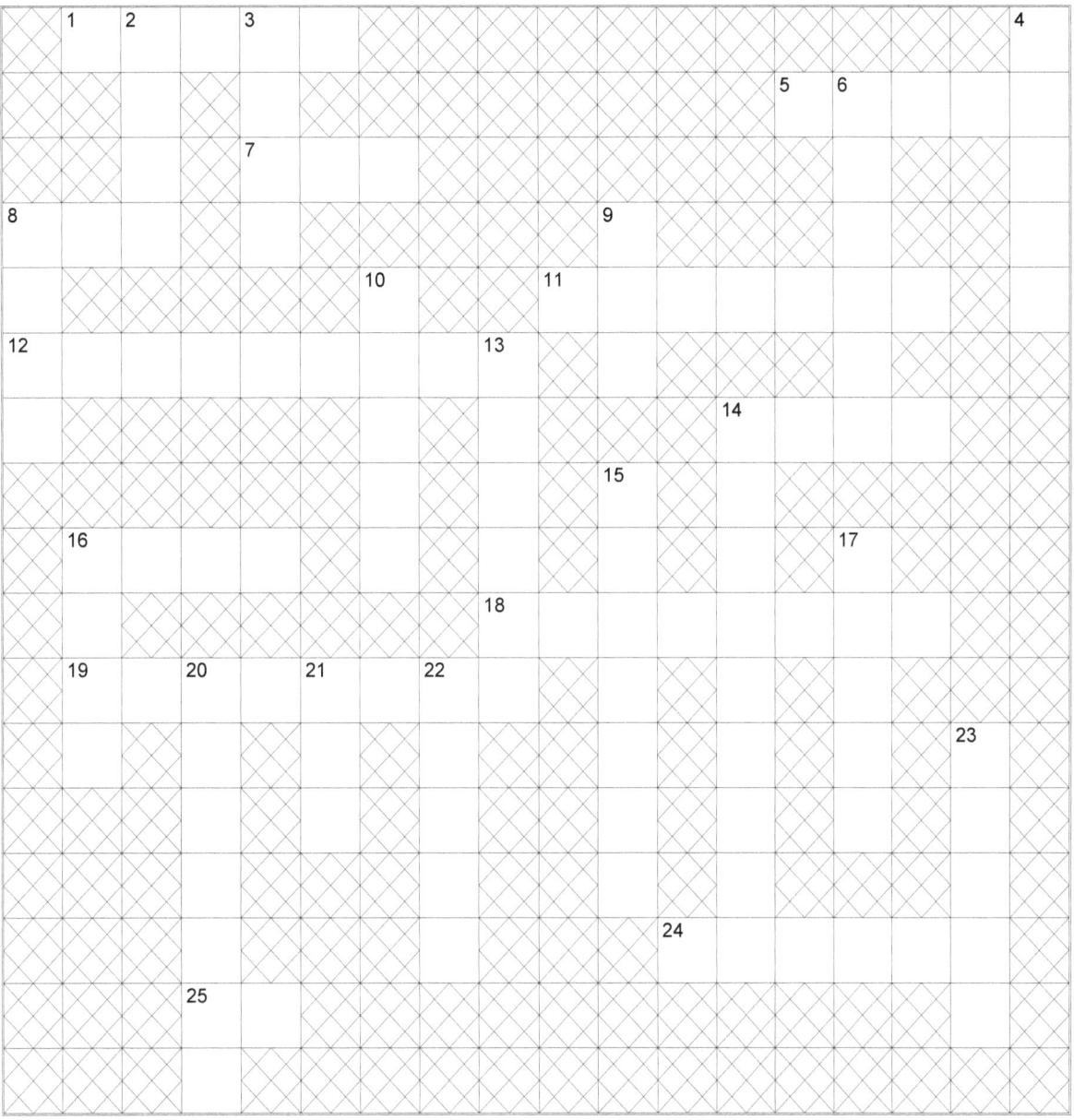

Across
1. Color of the light on the dock
5. So we beat on, _____ against the current ....
7. East or West _____
8. Daisy's husband
11. It took Gatsby three years to make the money to buy this
12. Business associate of Gatsby
14. Showed Gatsby how to live in the rich man's world
16. Narrator; Gatsby's neighbor
18. Gatsby had Jordan discuss this matter with Nick
19. It was in the Hopalong Casssidy book
24. Myrtle's husband
25. Initials of Gatsby's home state

Down
2. Wilson locked Myrtle in her _____
3. _____ of Dr. T.J. Eckleburg
4. Valley of _____; industrial zone
6. Gatsby told Nick he was educated there
8. Everything's so confused, let's all go to _____
9. Daisy runs into Myrtle with Gatsby's
10. Mr. Gatz; Gatsby's father
13. Tom's mistress
14. Myrtle's sister
15. Few people attended Gatsby's
16. Tom broke Myrtle's
17. Her voice is full of _____
20. Tom hates that word - even in kidding
21. What Mrs. Wilson bought while out with Tom and Nick
22. Gatsby wants Daisy to _____ Tom
23. Gatsby's real name

The Great Gatsby Crossword 4 Answer Key

	¹G	²R	³E	E	N							⁴A
		O	Y						⁵B	⁶O	A	T	S
		O	⁷E	G	G					X			H
⁸T	O	M	S			⁹C			F			E
O				¹⁰H		¹¹M	A	N	S	I	O	N	S
¹²W	O	L	F	S	H	E	I	M		R		R	
N					N	Y			¹⁴C	O	D	Y
					R	R		¹⁵F	A			
	¹⁶N	I	C	K	Y	T		U	T		¹⁷M	
	O					¹⁸L	U	N	C	H	E	O	N
	¹⁹S	²⁰C	²¹H	²²E	D	U	L	E		E		N	
	E	U		O		E		R		R		E	²³J
		L		G		A		A		I		Y	A
		K			V			L		N			M
		I		E			²⁴G	E	O	R	G	E
		²⁵N	D									S
		G										

Across
1. Color of the light on the dock
5. So we beat on, _____ against the current ....
7. East or West _____
8. Daisy's husband
11. It took Gatsby three years to make the money to buy this
12. Business associate of Gatsby
14. Showed Gatsby how to live in the rich man's world
16. Narrator; Gatsby's neighbor
18. Gatsby had Jordan discuss this matter with Nick
19. It was in the Hopalong Casssidy book
24. Myrtle's husband
25. Initials of Gatsby's home state

Down
2. Wilson locked Myrtle in her _____
3. _____ of Dr. T.J. Eckleburg
4. Valley of _____; industrial zone
6. Gatsby told Nick he was educated there
8. Everything's so confused, let's all go to _____
9. Daisy runs into Myrtle with Gatsby's
10. Mr. Gatz; Gatsby's father
13. Tom's mistress
14. Myrtle's sister
15. Few people attended Gatsby's
16. Tom broke Myrtle's
17. Her voice is full of _____
20. Tom hates that word - even in kidding
21. What Mrs. Wilson bought while out with Tom and Nick
22. Gatsby wants Daisy to _____ Tom
23. Gatsby's real name

The Great Gatsby

TOWN	BOATS	MIDWEST	JORDAN	TOM
JAMES	ASHES	OXFORD	GREEN	DOG
CATHERINE	FITZGERALD	FREE SPACE	DAISY	HULKING
CARRAWAY	ADVERTISEMENT	PARTIES	EGG	CARELESS
MONEY	CODY	WOLFSHEIM	ND	NICK

The Great Gatsby

COUSIN	INVITE	FUNERAL	APARTMENT	OWLEYES
NOSE	HENRY	EYES	LUNCHEON	LEAVE
ROOM	SCHEDULE	FREE SPACE	GATSBY	MANSION
MYRTLE	GEORGE	KILPSRINGER	NICK	ND
WOLFSHEIM	CODY	MONEY	CARELESS	EGG

The Great Gatsby

ADVERTISEMENT	KILPSPRINGER	NICK	TOM	GEORGE
JORDAN	MIDWEST	MONEY	DAISY	CATHERINE
ROOM	JAMES	FREE SPACE	CODY	EGG
HENRY	PAMMY	ND	OWLEYES	INVITE
DOG	ASHES	GATSBY	MYRTLE	TOWN

The Great Gatsby

SCHEDULE	WOLFSHEIM	FITZGERALD	FUNERAL	EYES
NOSE	OXFORD	GREEN	APARTMENT	PARTIES
LEAVE	LUNCHEON	FREE SPACE	CARRAWAY	MANSION
HULKING	COUSIN	CAR	TOWN	MYRTLE
GATSBY	ASHES	DOG	INVITE	OWLEYES

The Great Gatsby

CATHERINE	FITZGERALD	HULKING	GREEN	EGG
PAMMY	GATSBY	KILPSPRINGER	DAISY	TOWN
ADVERTISEMENT	BOATS	FREE SPACE	LUNCHEON	TOM
NICK	JAMES	DOG	PARTIES	SCHEDULE
EYES	OWLEYES	MYRTLE	INVITE	CAR

The Great Gatsby

CARRAWAY	MANSION	HENRY	CODY	COUSIN
GEORGE	FUNERAL	WOLFSHEIM	NOSE	MIDWEST
MONEY	LEAVE	FREE SPACE	ASHES	ROOM
APARTMENT	JORDAN	CARELESS	CAR	INVITE
MYRTLE	OWLEYES	EYES	SCHEDULE	PARTIES

The Great Gatsby

APARTMENT	NICK	DAISY	CATHERINE	BOATS
CARRAWAY	EYES	LEAVE	MIDWEST	SCHEDULE
TOM	TOWN	FREE SPACE	NOSE	PAMMY
MANSION	FITZGERALD	FUNERAL	ROOM	GREEN
INVITE	HULKING	MONEY	CAR	MYRTLE

The Great Gatsby

CARELESS	EGG	GEORGE	JORDAN	ND
LUNCHEON	OWLEYES	PARTIES	ASHES	JAMES
KILPSPRINGER	GATSBY	FREE SPACE	HENRY	WOLFSHEIM
OXFORD	COUSIN	DOG	MYRTLE	CAR
MONEY	HULKING	INVITE	GREEN	ROOM

The Great Gatsby

ROOM	WOLFSHEIM	CARRAWAY	FUNERAL	CAR
ASHES	ADVERTISEMENT	TOWN	CODY	DOG
KILPSPRINGER	APARTMENT	FREE SPACE	INVITE	DAISY
NICK	GATSBY	OXFORD	COUSIN	LUNCHEON
CARELESS	HULKING	PAMMY	BOATS	PARTIES

The Great Gatsby

MIDWEST	MONEY	GREEN	ND	JORDAN
MYRTLE	SCHEDULE	OWLEYES	GEORGE	HENRY
CATHERINE	LEAVE	FREE SPACE	TOM	NOSE
MANSION	JAMES	EYES	PARTIES	BOATS
PAMMY	HULKING	CARELESS	LUNCHEON	COUSIN

The Great Gatsby

ASHES	NOSE	WOLFSHEIM	HULKING	DOG
ND	FITZGERALD	JORDAN	LUNCHEON	GATSBY
JAMES	TOWN	FREE SPACE	BOATS	MONEY
CARELESS	CATHERINE	APARTMENT	LEAVE	OXFORD
MIDWEST	CARRAWAY	DAISY	INVITE	PAMMY

The Great Gatsby

PARTIES	SCHEDULE	OWLEYES	MYRTLE	CODY
GEORGE	NICK	GREEN	ROOM	EYES
CAR	COUSIN	FREE SPACE	EGG	FUNERAL
ADVERTISEMENT	TOM	MANSION	PAMMY	INVITE
DAISY	CARRAWAY	MIDWEST	OXFORD	LEAVE

The Great Gatsby

SCHEDULE	MYRTLE	LUNCHEON	FITZGERALD	GREEN
JORDAN	PARTIES	COUSIN	DOG	EYES
GATSBY	DAISY	FREE SPACE	TOWN	JAMES
CATHERINE	TOM	NOSE	ND	ROOM
KILPSPRINGER	CAR	APARTMENT	MANSION	HENRY

The Great Gatsby

NICK	ASHES	INVITE	OXFORD	ADVERTISEMENT
FUNERAL	HULKING	BOATS	OWLEYES	MONEY
PAMMY	CODY	FREE SPACE	GEORGE	MIDWEST
CARELESS	WOLFSHEIM	EGG	HENRY	MANSION
APARTMENT	CAR	KILPSPRINGER	ROOM	ND

The Great Gatsby

EYES	ROOM	OWLEYES	PAMMY	FITZGERALD
CATHERINE	ASHES	ADVERTISEMENT	MONEY	GREEN
MYRTLE	TOM	FREE SPACE	BOATS	NICK
HULKING	FUNERAL	HENRY	LUNCHEON	NOSE
PARTIES	CARELESS	CAR	JORDAN	SCHEDULE

The Great Gatsby

KILPSPRINGER	TOWN	INVITE	MIDWEST	CARRAWAY
MANSION	JAMES	WOLFSHEIM	ND	CODY
APARTMENT	EGG	FREE SPACE	COUSIN	OXFORD
DAISY	LEAVE	DOG	SCHEDULE	JORDAN
CAR	CARELESS	PARTIES	NOSE	LUNCHEON

The Great Gatsby

ASHES	GEORGE	CODY	GATSBY	LUNCHEON
KILPSPRINGER	TOWN	PARTIES	DAISY	DOG
HENRY	SCHEDULE	FREE SPACE	COUSIN	BOATS
NOSE	PAMMY	MIDWEST	INVITE	MYRTLE
CATHERINE	EGG	MONEY	MANSION	CARRAWAY

The Great Gatsby

OWLEYES	ADVERTISEMENT	ND	GREEN	JAMES
CAR	NICK	FUNERAL	HULKING	TOM
LEAVE	CARELESS	FREE SPACE	JORDAN	OXFORD
ROOM	EYES	APARTMENT	CARRAWAY	MANSION
MONEY	EGG	CATHERINE	MYRTLE	INVITE

The Great Gatsby

ASHES	COUSIN	EGG	NICK	FITZGERALD
MANSION	DAISY	HULKING	HENRY	TOM
MONEY	ND	FREE SPACE	FUNERAL	PARTIES
CARRAWAY	CARELESS	LUNCHEON	MIDWEST	BOATS
JAMES	SCHEDULE	GEORGE	WOLFSHEIM	DOG

The Great Gatsby

OXFORD	ROOM	ADVERTISEMENT	NOSE	CAR
KILPSPRINGER	PAMMY	GREEN	MYRTLE	EYES
CODY	CATHERINE	FREE SPACE	APARTMENT	LEAVE
JORDAN	OWLEYES	GATSBY	DOG	WOLFSHEIM
GEORGE	SCHEDULE	JAMES	BOATS	MIDWEST

The Great Gatsby

JAMES	PARTIES	FUNERAL	HENRY	CAR
TOWN	MANSION	EGG	INVITE	CARELESS
CATHERINE	EYES	FREE SPACE	CARRAWAY	OWLEYES
ADVERTISEMENT	GEORGE	BOATS	PAMMY	GATSBY
APARTMENT	MONEY	COUSIN	LEAVE	DOG

The Great Gatsby

LUNCHEON	FITZGERALD	ROOM	JORDAN	WOLFSHEIM
CODY	DAISY	TOM	HULKING	MYRTLE
NOSE	MIDWEST	FREE SPACE	GREEN	KILPSRINGER
ND	NICK	ASHES	DOG	LEAVE
COUSIN	MONEY	APARTMENT	GATSBY	PAMMY

The Great Gatsby

EYES	GEORGE	TOWN	MONEY	DAISY
APARTMENT	KILPSPRINGER	OXFORD	CATHERINE	OWLEYES
PARTIES	CARELESS	FREE SPACE	ASHES	GREEN
INVITE	HULKING	TOM	JORDAN	ROOM
LEAVE	EGG	COUSIN	CARRAWAY	FUNERAL

The Great Gatsby

ADVERTISEMENT	MANSION	NICK	HENRY	GATSBY
MYRTLE	CODY	CAR	ND	MIDWEST
NOSE	LUNCHEON	FREE SPACE	DOG	SCHEDULE
WOLFSHEIM	BOATS	FITZGERALD	FUNERAL	CARRAWAY
COUSIN	EGG	LEAVE	ROOM	JORDAN

The Great Gatsby

INVITE	CODY	FITZGERALD	HENRY	EYES
SCHEDULE	NICK	GEORGE	JAMES	GATSBY
APARTMENT	EGG	FREE SPACE	DOG	ASHES
KILPSPRINGER	HULKING	CARRAWAY	MANSION	NOSE
CATHERINE	COUSIN	CAR	MYRTLE	LUNCHEON

The Great Gatsby

MIDWEST	BOATS	FUNERAL	TOM	ADVERTISEMENT
ROOM	OWLEYES	PAMMY	GREEN	OXFORD
MONEY	DAISY	FREE SPACE	JORDAN	CARELESS
ND	TOWN	LEAVE	LUNCHEON	MYRTLE
CAR	COUSIN	CATHERINE	NOSE	MANSION

The Great Gatsby

PARTIES	MIDWEST	INVITE	NOSE	BOATS
MYRTLE	NICK	COUSIN	DOG	TOM
GREEN	FITZGERALD	FREE SPACE	ADVERTISEMENT	JORDAN
ROOM	FUNERAL	KILPSPRINGER	SCHEDULE	OXFORD
WOLFSHEIM	GEORGE	EYES	DAISY	LUNCHEON

The Great Gatsby

GATSBY	MONEY	CODY	CARRAWAY	APARTMENT
OWLEYES	HULKING	CATHERINE	ASHES	ND
PAMMY	HENRY	FREE SPACE	LEAVE	JAMES
CAR	EGG	MANSION	LUNCHEON	DAISY
EYES	GEORGE	WOLFSHEIM	OXFORD	SCHEDULE

The Great Gatsby

DOG	LUNCHEON	GEORGE	MYRTLE	CODY
EGG	MIDWEST	MONEY	APARTMENT	ND
HENRY	CATHERINE	FREE SPACE	ASHES	MANSION
DAISY	PARTIES	PAMMY	GATSBY	LEAVE
OWLEYES	HULKING	WOLFSHEIM	KILPSRINGER	JORDAN

The Great Gatsby

FUNERAL	NICK	TOM	OXFORD	JAMES
EYES	BOATS	INVITE	CARELESS	CAR
NOSE	FITZGERALD	FREE SPACE	CARRAWAY	GREEN
ROOM	SCHEDULE	TOWN	JORDAN	KILPSRINGER
WOLFSHEIM	HULKING	OWLEYES	LEAVE	GATSBY

The Great Gatsby

GREEN	GEORGE	SCHEDULE	LUNCHEON	NICK
OXFORD	CARELESS	MONEY	HULKING	NOSE
CAR	LEAVE	FREE SPACE	KILPSRINGER	DAISY
CATHERINE	BOATS	MYRTLE	JAMES	MANSION
HENRY	CODY	OWLEYES	DOG	APARTMENT

The Great Gatsby

ND	EYES	TOWN	EGG	ADVERTISEMENT
MIDWEST	ROOM	FITZGERALD	PAMMY	INVITE
JORDAN	COUSIN	FREE SPACE	ASHES	CARRAWAY
WOLFSHEIM	PARTIES	GATSBY	APARTMENT	DOG
OWLEYES	CODY	HENRY	MANSION	JAMES

The Great Gatsby Vocabulary Word List

No.	Word	Clue/Definition
1.	ADDENDA	Things that are added, esp. a supplement to a book
2.	AFFECTATIONS	A show, pretense or display
3.	AMORPHOUS	Lacking definite form
4.	CARAVANSARY	A large inn
5.	CATERWAULING	Shrill, discordant sound
6.	COMMENSURATE	Corresponding in size or degree
7.	CONTIGUOUS	Connecting without a break
8.	CONTINGENCY	Something incidental to something else
9.	CONVIVIAL	Merry; festive
10.	CORROBORATE	To strengthen or support with other evidence
11.	CORRUGATED	To shape into folds or parallel ridges and grooves
12.	DENIZEN	An inhabitant
13.	EPIGRAM	A short, witty poem
14.	ERRONEOUS	Mistaken
15.	EUPHEMISMS	The act of substituting a mild indirect term for a harsh, blunt or offensive one
16.	EXPOSTULATION	To dissuade or correct
17.	EXTEMPORIZING	To perform without prior preparation
18.	HAUTEUR	Haughtiness in bearing and attitude
19.	INCOHERENT	Unable to think in a clear or orderly manner
20.	INEXPLICABLE	Difficult to explain
21.	INNUENDO	An indirect usually derogatory implication in expression
22.	LABRYINTH	An intricate structure of interconnecting passages
23.	LIBERTINE	One who acts without moral restraint
24.	MERETRICIOUS	Attracting attention in a vulgar manner
25.	NEBULOUS	Cloudy, misty or hazy
26.	OBSTETRICAL	Care of a pregnant woman
27.	OMNIBUS	A long motor vehicle for passengers
28.	PANDERED	To act as a go-between in sexual intrigues
29.	PNEUMATIC	Relating to air or other gases
30.	PREEMPTORY	To take the place of
31.	PROVINCIAL	Limited in perspective
32.	RAJAH	A prince or chief
33.	RECEPTACLES	A container that holds items or matter
34.	REDOLENT	Suggestive
35.	RIVULETS	A small brook or stream
36.	ROTOGRAVURE	Printed material, such as a newspaper
37.	SCRUTINY	Close observation
38.	SOMNAMBULATORY	To walk in a sleeplike condition
39.	SUBTERFUGES	A deceptive stratagem or device
40.	SUPERCILIOUS	Feeling or showing haughty disdain
41.	TRAVERSED	To travel or pass across
42.	UNPUNCTUAL	Acting or arriving late for the appointed time

The Great Gatsby Vocabulary Fill In The Blank 1

_____ 1. Things that are added, esp. a supplement to a book

_____ 2. The act of substituting a mild indirect term for a harsh, blunt or offensive one

_____ 3. A container that holds items or matter

_____ 4. To walk in a sleeplike condition

_____ 5. One who acts without moral restraint

_____ 6. Acting or arriving late for the appointed time

_____ 7. A long motor vehicle for passengers

_____ 8. Lacking definite form

_____ 9. To perform without prior preparation

_____ 10. To dissuade or correct

_____ 11. An indirect usually derogatory implication in expression

_____ 12. A show, pretense or display

_____ 13. An inhabitant

_____ 14. Merry; festive

_____ 15. A small brook or stream

_____ 16. Feeling or showing haughty disdain

_____ 17. Something incidental to something else

_____ 18. Shrill, discordant sound

_____ 19. Cloudy, misty or hazy

_____ 20. Care of a pregnant woman

The Great Gatsby Vocabulary Fill In The Blank 1 Answer Key

ADDENDA	1. Things that are added, esp. a supplement to a book
EUPHEMISMS	2. The act of substituting a mild indirect term for a harsh, blunt or offensive one
RECEPTACLES	3. A container that holds items or matter
SOMNAMBULATORY	4. To walk in a sleeplike condition
LIBERTINE	5. One who acts without moral restraint
UNPUNCTUAL	6. Acting or arriving late for the appointed time
OMNIBUS	7. A long motor vehicle for passengers
AMORPHOUS	8. Lacking definite form
EXTEMPORIZING	9. To perform without prior preparation
EXPOSTULATION	10. To dissuade or correct
INNUENDO	11. An indirect usually derogatory implication in expression
AFFECTATIONS	12. A show, pretense or display
DENIZEN	13. An inhabitant
CONVIVIAL	14. Merry; festive
RIVULETS	15. A small brook or stream
SUPERCILIOUS	16. Feeling or showing haughty disdain
CONTINGENCY	17. Something incidental to something else
CATERWAULING	18. Shrill, discordant sound
NEBULOUS	19. Cloudy, misty or hazy
OBSTETRICAL	20. Care of a pregnant woman

The Great Gatsby Vocabulary Fill In The Blank 2

_____ 1. To take the place of

_____ 2. One who acts without moral restraint

_____ 3. Attracting attention in a vulgar manner

_____ 4. The act of substituting a mild indirect term for a harsh, blunt or offensive one

_____ 5. Unable to think in a clear or orderly manner

_____ 6. Limited in perspective

_____ 7. A long motor vehicle for passengers

_____ 8. Care of a pregnant woman

_____ 9. To strengthen or support with other evidence

_____ 10. An indirect usually derogatory implication in expression

_____ 11. To dissuade or correct

_____ 12. Cloudy, misty or hazy

_____ 13. To act as a go-between in sexual intrigues

_____ 14. Corresponding in size or degree

_____ 15. A small brook or stream

_____ 16. To perform without prior preparation

_____ 17. An inhabitant

_____ 18. A short, witty poem

_____ 19. To walk in a sleeplike condition

_____ 20. Shrill, discordant sound

The Great Gatsby Vocabulary Fill In The Blank 2 Answer Key

PREEMPTORY	1. To take the place of
LIBERTINE	2. One who acts without moral restraint
MERETRICIOUS	3. Attracting attention in a vulgar manner
EUPHEMISMS	4. The act of substituting a mild indirect term for a harsh, blunt or offensive one
INCOHERENT	5. Unable to think in a clear or orderly manner
PROVINCIAL	6. Limited in perspective
OMNIBUS	7. A long motor vehicle for passengers
OBSTETRICAL	8. Care of a pregnant woman
CORROBORATE	9. To strengthen or support with other evidence
INNUENDO	10. An indirect usually derogatory implication in expression
EXPOSTULATION	11. To dissuade or correct
NEBULOUS	12. Cloudy, misty or hazy
PANDERED	13. To act as a go-between in sexual intrigues
COMMENSURATE	14. Corresponding in size or degree
RIVULETS	15. A small brook or stream
EXTEMPORIZING	16. To perform without prior preparation
DENIZEN	17. An inhabitant
EPIGRAM	18. A short, witty poem
SOMNAMBULATORY	19. To walk in a sleeplike condition
CATERWAULING	20. Shrill, discordant sound

The Great Gatsby Vocabulary Fill In The Blank 3

1. Things that are added, esp. a supplement to a book
2. Unable to think in a clear or orderly manner
3. The act of substituting a mild indirect term for a harsh, blunt or offensive one
4. To strengthen or support with other evidence
5. A show, pretense or display
6. A container that holds items or matter
7. Something incidental to something else
8. An inhabitant
9. Mistaken
10. To travel or pass across
11. To walk in a sleeplike condition
12. Suggestive
13. Cloudy, misty or hazy
14. Acting or arriving late for the appointed time
15. Haughtiness in bearing and attitude
16. Difficult to explain
17. Limited in perspective
18. Attracting attention in a vulgar manner
19. Feeling or showing haughty disdain
20. A long motor vehicle for passengers

The Great Gatsby Vocabulary Fill In The Blank 3 Answer Key

ADDENDA	1. Things that are added, esp. a supplement to a book
INCOHERENT	2. Unable to think in a clear or orderly manner
EUPHEMISMS	3. The act of substituting a mild indirect term for a harsh, blunt or offensive one
CORROBORATE	4. To strengthen or support with other evidence
AFFECTATIONS	5. A show, pretense or display
RECEPTACLES	6. A container that holds items or matter
CONTINGENCY	7. Something incidental to something else
DENIZEN	8. An inhabitant
ERRONEOUS	9. Mistaken
TRAVERSED	10. To travel or pass across
SOMNAMBULATORY	11. To walk in a sleeplike condition
REDOLENT	12. Suggestive
NEBULOUS	13. Cloudy, misty or hazy
UNPUNCTUAL	14. Acting or arriving late for the appointed time
HAUTEUR	15. Haughtiness in bearing and attitude
INEXPLICABLE	16. Difficult to explain
PROVINCIAL	17. Limited in perspective
MERETRICIOUS	18. Attracting attention in a vulgar manner
SUPERCILIOUS	19. Feeling or showing haughty disdain
OMNIBUS	20. A long motor vehicle for passengers

The Great Gatsby Vocabulary Fill In The Blank 4

_____ 1. An indirect usually derogatory implication in expression

_____ 2. To perform without prior preparation

_____ 3. Printed material, such as a newspaper

_____ 4. A large inn

_____ 5. An inhabitant

_____ 6. Cloudy, misty or hazy

_____ 7. Haughtiness in bearing and attitude

_____ 8. To take the place of

_____ 9. A container that holds items or matter

_____ 10. One who acts without moral restraint

_____ 11. Attracting attention in a vulgar manner

_____ 12. A short, witty poem

_____ 13. To strengthen or support with other evidence

_____ 14. An intricate structure of interconnecting passages

_____ 15. Shrill, discordant sound

_____ 16. Lacking definite form

_____ 17. Care of a pregnant woman

_____ 18. A prince or chief

_____ 19. A deceptive stratagem or device

_____ 20. Acting or arriving late for the appointed time

The Great Gatsby Vocabulary Fill In The Blank 4 Answer Key

INNUENDO	1. An indirect usually derogatory implication in expression
EXTEMPORIZING	2. To perform without prior preparation
ROTOGRAVURE	3. Printed material, such as a newspaper
CARAVANSARY	4. A large inn
DENIZEN	5. An inhabitant
NEBULOUS	6. Cloudy, misty or hazy
HAUTEUR	7. Haughtiness in bearing and attitude
PREEMPTORY	8. To take the place of
RECEPTACLES	9. A container that holds items or matter
LIBERTINE	10. One who acts without moral restraint
MERETRICIOUS	11. Attracting attention in a vulgar manner
EPIGRAM	12. A short, witty poem
CORROBORATE	13. To strengthen or support with other evidence
LABRYINTH	14. An intricate structure of interconnecting passages
CATERWAULING	15. Shrill, discordant sound
AMORPHOUS	16. Lacking definite form
OBSTETRICAL	17. Care of a pregnant woman
RAJAH	18. A prince or chief
SUBTERFUGES	19. A deceptive stratagem or device
UNPUNCTUAL	20. Acting or arriving late for the appointed time

The Great Gatsby Vocabulary Matching 1

___ 1. ROTOGRAVURE   A. To act as a go-between in sexual intrigues
___ 2. ADDENDA   B. Something incidental to something else
___ 3. AMORPHOUS   C. Care of a pregnant woman
___ 4. NEBULOUS   D. Mistaken
___ 5. INCOHERENT   E. Cloudy, misty or hazy
___ 6. PREEMPTORY   F. Unable to think in a clear or orderly manner
___ 7. CONTINGENCY   G. Suggestive
___ 8. RAJAH   H. To strengthen or support with other evidence
___ 9. CORROBORATE   I. Printed material, such as a newspaper
___10. RIVULETS   J. Relating to air or other gases
___11. AFFECTATIONS   K. To dissuade or correct
___12. INEXPLICABLE   L. Shrill, discordant sound
___13. PNEUMATIC   M. Things that are added, esp. a supplement to a book
___14. CATERWAULING   N. One who acts without moral restraint
___15. MERETRICIOUS   O. Difficult to explain
___16. SUPERCILIOUS   P. A small brook or stream
___17. CORRUGATED   Q. To take the place of
___18. EXPOSTULATION   R. To shape into folds or parallel ridges and grooves
___19. ERRONEOUS   S. Feeling or showing haughty disdain
___20. PANDERED   T. A large inn
___21. CARAVANSARY   U. Lacking definite form
___22. COMMENSURATE   V. Corresponding in size or degree
___23. REDOLENT   W. A prince or chief
___24. OBSTETRICAL   X. Attracting attention in a vulgar manner
___25. LIBERTINE   Y. A show, pretense or display

The Great Gatsby Vocabulary Matching 1 Answer Key

I - 1. ROTOGRAVURE	A.	To act as a go-between in sexual intrigues
M - 2. ADDENDA	B.	Something incidental to something else
U - 3. AMORPHOUS	C.	Care of a pregnant woman
E - 4. NEBULOUS	D.	Mistaken
F - 5. INCOHERENT	E.	Cloudy, misty or hazy
Q - 6. PREEMPTORY	F.	Unable to think in a clear or orderly manner
B - 7. CONTINGENCY	G.	Suggestive
W - 8. RAJAH	H.	To strengthen or support with other evidence
H - 9. CORROBORATE	I.	Printed material, such as a newspaper
P - 10. RIVULETS	J.	Relating to air or other gases
Y - 11. AFFECTATIONS	K.	To dissuade or correct
O - 12. INEXPLICABLE	L.	Shrill, discordant sound
J - 13. PNEUMATIC	M.	Things that are added, esp. a supplement to a book
L - 14. CATERWAULING	N.	One who acts without moral restraint
X - 15. MERETRICIOUS	O.	Difficult to explain
S - 16. SUPERCILIOUS	P.	A small brook or stream
R - 17. CORRUGATED	Q.	To take the place of
K - 18. EXPOSTULATION	R.	To shape into folds or parallel ridges and grooves
D - 19. ERRONEOUS	S.	Feeling or showing haughty disdain
A - 20. PANDERED	T.	A large inn
T - 21. CARAVANSARY	U.	Lacking definite form
V - 22. COMMENSURATE	V.	Corresponding in size or degree
G - 23. REDOLENT	W.	A prince or chief
C - 24. OBSTETRICAL	X.	Attracting attention in a vulgar manner
N - 25. LIBERTINE	Y.	A show, pretense or display

The Great Gatsby Vocabulary Matching 2

___ 1. RIVULETS   A. A large inn
___ 2. CARAVANSARY   B. Shrill, discordant sound
___ 3. SUBTERFUGES   C. A prince or chief
___ 4. UNPUNCTUAL   D. Care of a pregnant woman
___ 5. ADDENDA   E. Lacking definite form
___ 6. OMNIBUS   F. Mistaken
___ 7. EUPHEMISMS   G. Acting or arriving late for the appointed time
___ 8. OBSTETRICAL   H. A deceptive stratagem or device
___ 9. ERRONEOUS   I. To perform without prior preparation
___10. SCRUTINY   J. An indirect usually derogatory implication in expression
___11. PNEUMATIC   K. Things that are added, esp. a supplement to a book
___12. INNUENDO   L. The act of substituting a mild indirect term for a harsh, blunt or offensive one
___13. CORRUGATED   M. To dissuade or correct
___14. AMORPHOUS   N. Printed material, such as a newspaper
___15. TRAVERSED   O. A small brook or stream
___16. LABRYINTH   P. Difficult to explain
___17. EXTEMPORIZING   Q. To shape into folds or parallel ridges and grooves
___18. INEXPLICABLE   R. An inhabitant
___19. RAJAH   S. A long motor vehicle for passengers
___20. ROTOGRAVURE   T. Cloudy, misty or hazy
___21. DENIZEN   U. Relating to air or other gases
___22. EXPOSTULATION   V. To travel or pass across
___23. NEBULOUS   W. Close observation
___24. CATERWAULING   X. Unable to think in a clear or orderly manner
___25. INCOHERENT   Y. An intricate structure of interconnecting passages

The Great Gatsby Vocabulary Matching 2 Answer Key

O - 1. RIVULETS	A.	A large inn
A - 2. CARAVANSARY	B.	Shrill, discordant sound
H - 3. SUBTERFUGES	C.	A prince or chief
G - 4. UNPUNCTUAL	D.	Care of a pregnant woman
K - 5. ADDENDA	E.	Lacking definite form
S - 6. OMNIBUS	F.	Mistaken
L - 7. EUPHEMISMS	G.	Acting or arriving late for the appointed time
D - 8. OBSTETRICAL	H.	A deceptive stratagem or device
F - 9. ERRONEOUS	I.	To perform without prior preparation
W -10. SCRUTINY	J.	An indirect usually derogatory implication in expression
U -11. PNEUMATIC	K.	Things that are added, esp. a supplement to a book
J - 12. INNUENDO	L.	The act of substituting a mild indirect term for a harsh, blunt or offensive one
Q -13. CORRUGATED	M.	To dissuade or correct
E -14. AMORPHOUS	N.	Printed material, such as a newspaper
V -15. TRAVERSED	O.	A small brook or stream
Y -16. LABRYINTH	P.	Difficult to explain
I - 17. EXTEMPORIZING	Q.	To shape into folds or parallel ridges and grooves
P -18. INEXPLICABLE	R.	An inhabitant
C -19. RAJAH	S.	A long motor vehicle for passengers
N -20. ROTOGRAVURE	T.	Cloudy, misty or hazy
R -21. DENIZEN	U.	Relating to air or other gases
M -22. EXPOSTULATION	V.	To travel or pass across
T -23. NEBULOUS	W.	Close observation
B -24. CATERWAULING	X.	Unable to think in a clear or orderly manner
X -25. INCOHERENT	Y.	An intricate structure of interconnecting passages

The Great Gatsby Vocabulary Matching 3

___ 1. HAUTEUR A. To walk in a sleeplike condition
___ 2. CARAVANSARY B. To take the place of
___ 3. PREEMPTORY C. One who acts without moral restraint
___ 4. DENIZEN D. A large inn
___ 5. LABRYINTH E. Things that are added, esp. a supplement to a book
___ 6. SOMNAMBULATORY F. The act of substituting a mild indirect term for a harsh, blunt or offensive one
___ 7. MERETRICIOUS G. Attracting attention in a vulgar manner
___ 8. SCRUTINY H. Limited in perspective
___ 9. EUPHEMISMS I. Suggestive
___10. EPIGRAM J. Feeling or showing haughty disdain
___11. PNEUMATIC K. An indirect usually derogatory implication in expression
___12. AFFECTATIONS L. Difficult to explain
___13. ADDENDA M. Shrill, discordant sound
___14. CORROBORATE N. Haughtiness in bearing and attitude
___15. INEXPLICABLE O. Relating to air or other gases
___16. SUPERCILIOUS P. An intricate structure of interconnecting passages
___17. LIBERTINE Q. Printed material, such as a newspaper
___18. AMORPHOUS R. A short, witty poem
___19. REDOLENT S. Close observation
___20. OMNIBUS T. To strengthen or support with other evidence
___21. EXTEMPORIZING U. A show, pretense or display
___22. PROVINCIAL V. A long motor vehicle for passengers
___23. INNUENDO W. To perform without prior preparation
___24. ROTOGRAVURE X. Lacking definite form
___25. CATERWAULING Y. An inhabitant

The Great Gatsby Vocabulary Matching 3 Answer Key

N - 1. HAUTEUR
D - 2. CARAVANSARY
B - 3. PREEMPTORY
Y - 4. DENIZEN
P - 5. LABRYINTH
A - 6. SOMNAMBULATORY
G - 7. MERETRICIOUS
S - 8. SCRUTINY
F - 9. EUPHEMISMS
R - 10. EPIGRAM
O - 11. PNEUMATIC
U - 12. AFFECTATIONS
E - 13. ADDENDA
T - 14. CORROBORATE
L - 15. INEXPLICABLE
J - 16. SUPERCILIOUS
C - 17. LIBERTINE
X - 18. AMORPHOUS
I - 19. REDOLENT
V - 20. OMNIBUS
W - 21. EXTEMPORIZING
H - 22. PROVINCIAL
K - 23. INNUENDO
Q - 24. ROTOGRAVURE
M - 25. CATERWAULING

A. To walk in a sleeplike condition
B. To take the place of
C. One who acts without moral restraint
D. A large inn
E. Things that are added, esp. a supplement to a book
F. The act of substituting a mild indirect term for a harsh, blunt or offensive one
G. Attracting attention in a vulgar manner
H. Limited in perspective
I. Suggestive
J. Feeling or showing haughty disdain
K. An indirect usually derogatory implication in expression
L. Difficult to explain
M. Shrill, discordant sound
N. Haughtiness in bearing and attitude
O. Relating to air or other gases
P. An intricate structure of interconnecting passages
Q. Printed material, such as a newspaper
R. A short, witty poem
S. Close observation
T. To strengthen or support with other evidence
U. A show, pretense or display
V. A long motor vehicle for passengers
W. To perform without prior preparation
X. Lacking definite form
Y. An inhabitant

The Great Gatsby Vocabulary Matching 4

___ 1. EPIGRAM
___ 2. ROTOGRAVURE
___ 3. DENIZEN
___ 4. INCOHERENT
___ 5. RECEPTACLES
___ 6. PANDERED
___ 7. OBSTETRICAL
___ 8. COMMENSURATE
___ 9. NEBULOUS
___ 10. CATERWAULING
___ 11. SCRUTINY
___ 12. UNPUNCTUAL
___ 13. CORROBORATE
___ 14. TRAVERSED
___ 15. EUPHEMISMS
___ 16. REDOLENT
___ 17. INNUENDO
___ 18. CARAVANSARY
___ 19. AFFECTATIONS
___ 20. RAJAH
___ 21. CONVIVIAL
___ 22. CORRUGATED
___ 23. CONTIGUOUS
___ 24. LIBERTINE
___ 25. PNEUMATIC

A. Shrill, discordant sound
B. Connecting without a break
C. To act as a go-between in sexual intrigues
D. To strengthen or support with other evidence
E. Relating to air or other gases
F. Care of a pregnant woman
G. To travel or pass across
H. A show, pretense or display
I. The act of substituting a mild indirect term for a harsh, blunt or offensive one
J. Printed material, such as a newspaper
K. A large inn
L. An indirect usually derogatory implication in expression
M. An inhabitant
N. Cloudy, misty or hazy
O. A container that holds items or matter
P. Merry; festive
Q. Suggestive
R. A short, witty poem
S. Unable to think in a clear or orderly manner
T. One who acts without moral restraint
U. A prince or chief
V. Close observation
W. To shape into folds or parallel ridges and grooves
X. Corresponding in size or degree
Y. Acting or arriving late for the appointed time

The Great Gatsby Vocabulary Matching 4 Answer Key

R - 1.	EPIGRAM	A. Shrill, discordant sound
J - 2.	ROTOGRAVURE	B. Connecting without a break
M - 3.	DENIZEN	C. To act as a go-between in sexual intrigues
S - 4.	INCOHERENT	D. To strengthen or support with other evidence
O - 5.	RECEPTACLES	E. Relating to air or other gases
C - 6.	PANDERED	F. Care of a pregnant woman
F - 7.	OBSTETRICAL	G. To travel or pass across
X - 8.	COMMENSURATE	H. A show, pretense or display
N - 9.	NEBULOUS	I. The act of substituting a mild indirect term for a harsh, blunt or offensive one
A - 10.	CATERWAULING	J. Printed material, such as a newspaper
V - 11.	SCRUTINY	K. A large inn
Y - 12.	UNPUNCTUAL	L. An indirect usually derogatory implication in expression
D - 13.	CORROBORATE	M. An inhabitant
G - 14.	TRAVERSED	N. Cloudy, misty or hazy
I - 15.	EUPHEMISMS	O. A container that holds items or matter
Q - 16.	REDOLENT	P. Merry; festive
L - 17.	INNUENDO	Q. Suggestive
K - 18.	CARAVANSARY	R. A short, witty poem
H - 19.	AFFECTATIONS	S. Unable to think in a clear or orderly manner
U - 20.	RAJAH	T. One who acts without moral restraint
P - 21.	CONVIVIAL	U. A prince or chief
W - 22.	CORRUGATED	V. Close observation
B - 23.	CONTIGUOUS	W. To shape into folds or parallel ridges and grooves
T - 24.	LIBERTINE	X. Corresponding in size or degree
E - 25.	PNEUMATIC	Y. Acting or arriving late for the appointed time

The Great Gatsby Vocabulary Magic Squares 1

Match the definition with the vocabulary word. Put your answers in the magic squares below. When your answers are correct, all columns and rows will add to the same number.

A. CARAVANSARY
B. HAUTEUR
C. ADDENDA
D. SUBTERFUGES
E. PNEUMATIC
F. PANDERED
G. CATERWAULING
H. TRAVERSED
I. CONVIVIAL
J. ROTOGRAVURE
K. AFFECTATIONS
L. INNUENDO
M. PREEMPTORY
N. INEXPLICABLE
O. REDOLENT
P. PROVINCIAL

1. Haughtiness in bearing and attitude
2. Shrill, discordant sound
3. A show, pretense or display
4. Difficult to explain
5. To take the place of
6. An indirect usually derogatory implication in expression
7. To travel or pass across
8. A large inn
9. Limited in perspective
10. Merry; festive
11. Relating to air or other gases
12. A deceptive stratagem or device
13. Things that are added, esp. a supplement to a book
14. To act as a go-between in sexual intrigues
15. Printed material, such as a newspaper
16. Suggestive

A=	B=	C=	D=
E=	F=	G=	H=
I=	J=	K=	L=
M=	N=	O=	P=

The Great Gatsby Vocabulary Magic Squares 1 Answer Key

Match the definition with the vocabulary word. Put your answers in the magic squares below. When your answers are correct, all columns and rows will add to the same number.

A. CARAVANSARY
B. HAUTEUR
C. ADDENDA
D. SUBTERFUGES
E. PNEUMATIC
F. PANDERED
G. CATERWAULING
H. TRAVERSED
I. CONVIVIAL
J. ROTOGRAVURE
K. AFFECTATIONS
L. INNUENDO
M. PREEMPTORY
N. INEXPLICABLE
O. REDOLENT
P. PROVINCIAL

1. Haughtiness in bearing and attitude
2. Shrill, discordant sound
3. A show, pretense or display
4. Difficult to explain
5. To take the place of
6. An indirect usually derogatory implication in expression
7. To travel or pass across
8. A large inn
9. Limited in perspective
10. Merry; festive
11. Relating to air or other gases
12. A deceptive stratagem or device
13. Things that are added, esp. a supplement to a book
14. To act as a go-between in sexual intrigues
15. Printed material, such as a newspaper
16. Suggestive

A=8	B=1	C=13	D=12
E=11	F=14	G=2	H=7
I=10	J=15	K=3	L=6
M=5	N=4	O=16	P=9

The Great Gatsby Vocabulary Magic Squares 2

Match the definition with the vocabulary word. Put your answers in the magic squares below. When your answers are correct, all columns and rows will add to the same number.

A. INNUENDO
B. CORROBORATE
C. LIBERTINE
D. NEBULOUS
E. EXTEMPORIZING
F. REDOLENT
G. INCOHERENT
H. PNEUMATIC
I. SCRUTINY
J. CORRUGATED
K. AFFECTATIONS
L. ROTOGRAVURE
M. CONVIVIAL
N. SUPERCILIOUS
O. TRAVERSED
P. CARAVANSARY

1. To travel or pass across
2. To shape into folds or parallel ridges and grooves
3. Relating to air or other gases
4. An indirect usually derogatory implication in expression
5. Cloudy, misty or hazy
6. To perform without prior preparation
7. A show, pretense or display
8. Feeling or showing haughty disdain
9. Suggestive
10. One who acts without moral restraint
11. Merry; festive
12. Printed material, such as a newspaper
13. Close observation
14. A large inn
15. To strengthen or support with other evidence
16. Unable to think in a clear or orderly manner

A=	B=	C=	D=
E=	F=	G=	H=
I=	J=	K=	L=
M=	N=	O=	P=

The Great Gatsby Vocabulary Magic Squares 2 Answer Key

Match the definition with the vocabulary word. Put your answers in the magic squares below. When your answers are correct, all columns and rows will add to the same number.

A. INNUENDO
B. CORROBORATE
C. LIBERTINE
D. NEBULOUS
E. EXTEMPORIZING
F. REDOLENT
G. INCOHERENT
H. PNEUMATIC
I. SCRUTINY
J. CORRUGATED
K. AFFECTATIONS
L. ROTOGRAVURE
M. CONVIVIAL
N. SUPERCILIOUS
O. TRAVERSED
P. CARAVANSARY

1. To travel or pass across
2. To shape into folds or parallel ridges and grooves
3. Relating to air or other gases
4. An indirect usually derogatory implication in expression
5. Cloudy, misty or hazy
6. To perform without prior preparation
7. A show, pretense or display
8. Feeling or showing haughty disdain
9. Suggestive
10. One who acts without moral restraint
11. Merry; festive
12. Printed material, such as a newspaper
13. Close observation
14. A large inn
15. To strengthen or support with other evidence
16. Unable to think in a clear or orderly manner

A=4	B=15	C=10	D=5
E=6	F=9	G=16	H=3
I=13	J=2	K=7	L=12
M=11	N=8	O=1	P=14

The Great Gatsby Vocabulary Magic Squares 3

Match the definition with the vocabulary word. Put your answers in the magic squares below. When your answers are correct, all columns and rows will add to the same number.

A. INCOHERENT
B. EXTEMPORIZING
C. CARAVANSARY
D. MERETRICIOUS
E. PANDERED
F. PNEUMATIC
G. CONTINGENCY
H. OBSTETRICAL
I. CORROBORATE
J. HAUTEUR
K. SOMNAMBULATORY
L. EPIGRAM
M. LABRYINTH
N. COMMENSURATE
O. AMORPHOUS
P. NEBULOUS

1. An intricate structure of interconnecting passages
2. Relating to air or other gases
3. Care of a pregnant woman
4. Lacking definite form
5. A short, witty poem
6. A large inn
7. Unable to think in a clear or orderly manner
8. Haughtiness in bearing and attitude
9. To walk in a sleeplike condition
10. Attracting attention in a vulgar manner
11. To perform without prior preparation
12. To strengthen or support with other evidence
13. Corresponding in size or degree
14. To act as a go-between in sexual intrigues
15. Something incidental to something else
16. Cloudy, misty or hazy

A=	B=	C=	D=
E=	F=	G=	H=
I=	J=	K=	L=
M=	N=	O=	P=

The Great Gatsby Vocabulary Magic Squares 3 Answer Key

Match the definition with the vocabulary word. Put your answers in the magic squares below. When your answers are correct, all columns and rows will add to the same number.

A. INCOHERENT
B. EXTEMPORIZING
C. CARAVANSARY
D. MERETRICIOUS
E. PANDERED
F. PNEUMATIC
G. CONTINGENCY
H. OBSTETRICAL
I. CORROBORATE
J. HAUTEUR
K. SOMNAMBULATORY
L. EPIGRAM
M. LABRYINTH
N. COMMENSURATE
O. AMORPHOUS
P. NEBULOUS

1. An intricate structure of interconnecting passages
2. Relating to air or other gases
3. Care of a pregnant woman
4. Lacking definite form
5. A short, witty poem
6. A large inn
7. Unable to think in a clear or orderly manner
8. Haughtiness in bearing and attitude
9. To walk in a sleeplike condition
10. Attracting attention in a vulgar manner
11. To perform without prior preparation
12. To strengthen or support with other evidence
13. Corresponding in size or degree
14. To act as a go-between in sexual intrigues
15. Something incidental to something else
16. Cloudy, misty or hazy

A=7	B=11	C=6	D=10
E=14	F=2	G=15	H=3
I=12	J=8	K=9	L=5
M=1	N=13	O=4	P=16

The Great Gatsby Vocabulary Magic Squares 4

Match the definition with the vocabulary word. Put your answers in the magic squares below. When your answers are correct, all columns and rows will add to the same number.

A. CATERWAULING   G. EPIGRAM   M. ERRONEOUS
B. SCRUTINY   H. COMMENSURATE   N. EXTEMPORIZING
C. REDOLENT   I. CONVIVIAL   O. INNUENDO
D. UNPUNCTUAL   J. SOMNAMBULATORY   P. AMORPHOUS
E. CONTINGENCY   K. NEBULOUS
F. AFFECTATIONS   L. TRAVERSED

1. Shrill, discordant sound
2. To perform without prior preparation
3. To walk in a sleeplike condition
4. Something incidental to something else
5. A short, witty poem
6. To travel or pass across
7. Lacking definite form
8. Suggestive
9. An indirect usually derogatory implication in expression
10. Acting or arriving late for the appointed time
11. Corresponding in size or degree
12. Cloudy, misty or hazy
13. Merry; festive
14. A show, pretense or display
15. Close observation
16. Mistaken

A=	B=	C=	D=
E=	F=	G=	H=
I=	J=	K=	L=
M=	N=	O=	P=

The Great Gatsby Vocabulary Magic Squares 4 Answer Key

Match the definition with the vocabulary word. Put your answers in the magic squares below. When your answers are correct, all columns and rows will add to the same number.

A. CATERWAULING
B. SCRUTINY
C. REDOLENT
D. UNPUNCTUAL
E. CONTINGENCY
F. AFFECTATIONS
G. EPIGRAM
H. COMMENSURATE
I. CONVIVIAL
J. SOMNAMBULATORY
K. NEBULOUS
L. TRAVERSED
M. ERRONEOUS
N. EXTEMPORIZING
O. INNUENDO
P. AMORPHOUS

1. Shrill, discordant sound
2. To perform without prior preparation
3. To walk in a sleeplike condition
4. Something incidental to something else
5. A short, witty poem
6. To travel or pass across
7. Lacking definite form
8. Suggestive
9. An indirect usually derogatory implication in expression
10. Acting or arriving late for the appointed time
11. Corresponding in size or degree
12. Cloudy, misty or hazy
13. Merry; festive
14. A show, pretense or display
15. Close observation
16. Mistaken

A=1	B=15	C=8	D=10
E=4	F=14	G=5	H=11
I=13	J=3	K=12	L=6
M=16	N=2	O=9	P=7

The Great Gatsby Vocabulary Word Search 1

```
P L W Q A V X X N W J H C Q T S S C T F
A A T H D C X E M V Z A P R B C S O X L
N B N W D G Z K P N L U X D X R M R B T
D R E I E I M R L B S T T E E U S R Q G
E Y L C N M X A A F F E C T A T I O N S
R I O E D C I J P D R U A A K I M B U U
E N D B A V O A L R Y R J G Q N E O N B
D T E I I M T H O X U C T U C Y H R E T
G H R V N L S N E S W B Y R Q P P A B E
N R N I V E E F N R L R Z R R O U T U R
S O B Q C O X E M Y E Y V O M B E E L F
C U M P U A M P D E R N M C C S X P O U
S I P S R M R G L O R A T D B T Y I U G
R N P E O O X A T I V E E W E E C G S E
O N Q C R P V P V H C S T M F T N R C S
T U K H E C M I K A R A P R N R E A O D
O E F P C E I X N E N O B C I I G M N D
G N W M E W Z L V C R S I L S C N F T G
R D Y R P H D A I I I T A T E A I F I W
A O P Z T M R K Z O A A E R M L T O G Z
V K Z Y A T Z I N M U L L Z Y Q N G U C
U C L T C N N H U R U S C D W T O G O S
R Y B P L G V E L V P H T L W L C H U W
E T Q R E R N P I L I B E R T I N E S S
D V D W S P F R C A T E R W A U L I N G
```

A container that holds items or matter (11)
A deceptive stratagem or device (11)
A large inn (11)
A long motor vehicle for passengers (7)
A prince or chief (5)
A short, witty poem (7)
A show, pretense or display (12)
A small brook or stream (8)
An indirect usually derogatory implication in expression (8)
An inhabitant (7)
An intricate structure of interconnecting passages (9)
Attracting attention in a vulgar manner (12)
Care of a pregnant woman (11)
Close observation (8)
Cloudy, misty or hazy (8)
Connecting without a break (10)
Corresponding in size or degree (12)
Difficult to explain (12)
Feeling or showing haughty disdain (12)
Haughtiness in bearing and attitude (7)
Lacking definite form (9)

Limited in perspective (10)
Merry; festive (9)
Mistaken (9)
One who acts without moral restraint (9)
Printed material, such as a newspaper (11)
Relating to air or other gases (9)
Shrill, discordant sound (12)
Something incidental to something else (11)
Suggestive (8)
The act of substituting a mild indirect term for a harsh, blunt or offensive one (10)
Things that are added, esp. a supplement to a book (7)
To act as a go-between in sexual intrigues (8)
To perform without prior preparation (13)
To shape into folds or parallel ridges and grooves (10)
To strengthen or support with other evidence (11)
To take the place of (10)
To travel or pass across (9)
Unable to think in a clear or orderly manner (10)

The Great Gatsby Vocabulary Word Search 1 Answer Key

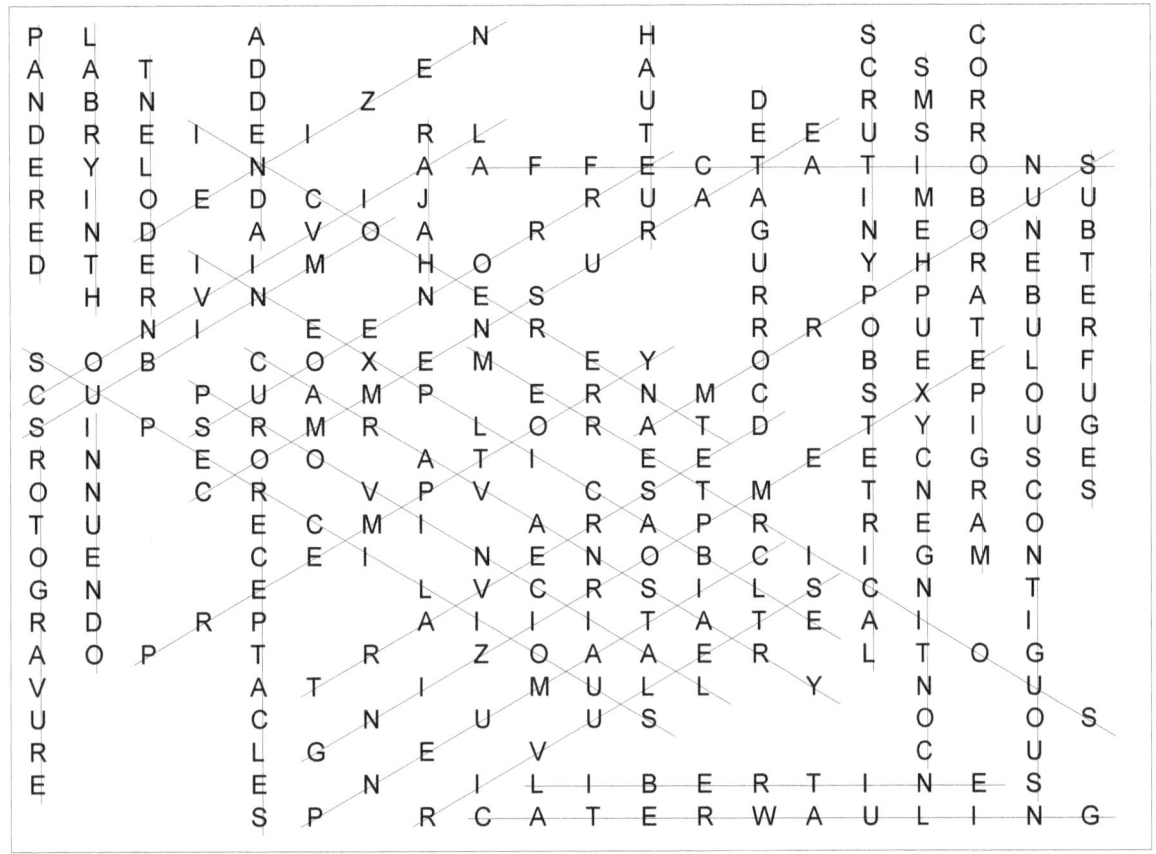

- A container that holds items or matter (11)
- A deceptive stratagem or device (11)
- A large inn (11)
- A long motor vehicle for passengers (7)
- A prince or chief (5)
- A short, witty poem (7)
- A show, pretense or display (12)
- A small brook or stream (8)
- An indirect usually derogatory implication in expression (8)
- An inhabitant (7)
- An intricate structure of interconnecting passages (9)
- Attracting attention in a vulgar manner (12)
- Care of a pregnant woman (11)
- Close observation (8)
- Cloudy, misty or hazy (8)
- Connecting without a break (10)
- Corresponding in size or degree (12)
- Difficult to explain (12)
- Feeling or showing haughty disdain (12)
- Haughtiness in bearing and attitude (7)
- Lacking definite form (9)
- Limited in perspective (10)
- Merry; festive (9)
- Mistaken (9)
- One who acts without moral restraint (9)
- Printed material, such as a newspaper (11)
- Relating to air or other gases (9)
- Shrill, discordant sound (12)
- Something incidental to something else (11)
- Suggestive (8)
- The act of substituting a mild indirect term for a harsh, blunt or offensive one (10)
- Things that are added, esp. a supplement to a book (7)
- To act as a go-between in sexual intrigues (8)
- To perform without prior preparation (13)
- To shape into folds or parallel ridges and grooves (10)
- To strengthen or support with other evidence (11)
- To take the place of (10)
- To travel or pass across (9)
- Unable to think in a clear or orderly manner (10)

The Great Gatsby Vocabulary Word Search 2

```
L V M A F S L H L N X N L T F C R T I Y
Q C T R M T T A C V X L B Y S O Y R N V
Q M X S G O B M R H V Z H C C M X E E C
T D T U G R R Q X N S S A N R M W D X J
N F F B Y C B P V G U Z U E U E C O P B
E N Q I W W L N H O L L T G T N L L L L
R X N N E X W Y I O K Y E N I S D E I X
E T J M Q P C C D D U N U I N U E N C V
H R C O N T I G U O U S R T Y R W T A G
O P A T K R T G H B M U L N R A U D B Z
C A P J T P A X R S G B H O B T N C L C
N N Y E A C M C I A J T N C H E P A E S
I D R J C H U M N L M E R F D D U T I B
C E O G J O E T M E O R Z D E C N E N B
M R T E N H N X R U B F A T G K C R N K
K E P R P T P V S E W U A W S Z T W U F
J D M U D R B K I Y C G L N V S U A E C
X V E V E A P Q F V U E V O T F A U N Q
P Z E A N V T R H R I S P E U N L L D M
D Y R R I E S F R B X A L T V S L I O M
K P P G Z R H O K P V U L N A D Q N X C
G F C O E S C L R L V X C J W C J G N Z
X S G T N E B Y W I Q B X P R J L P P D
F Z G O N D D Z R L I B E R T I N E N T
Y K D R O B S T E T R I C A L T B C S B
```

A container that holds items or matter (11)
A deceptive stratagem or device (11)
A long motor vehicle for passengers (7)
A prince or chief (5)
A short, witty poem (7)
A small brook or stream (8)
Acting or arriving late for the appointed time (10)
An indirect usually derogatory implication in expression (8)
An inhabitant (7)
An intricate structure of interconnecting passages (9)
Attracting attention in a vulgar manner (12)
Care of a pregnant woman (11)
Close observation (8)
Cloudy, misty or hazy (8)
Connecting without a break (10)
Corresponding in size or degree (12)
Difficult to explain (12)
Haughtiness in bearing and attitude (7)
Lacking definite form (9)
Merry; festive (9)

Mistaken (9)
One who acts without moral restraint (9)
Printed material, such as a newspaper (11)
Relating to air or other gases (9)
Shrill, discordant sound (12)
Something incidental to something else (11)
Suggestive (8)
The act of substituting a mild indirect term for a harsh, blunt or offensive one (10)
Things that are added, esp. a supplement to a book (7)
To act as a go-between in sexual intrigues (8)
To shape into folds or parallel ridges and grooves (10)
To take the place of (10)
To travel or pass across (9)
Unable to think in a clear or orderly manner (10)

The Great Gatsby Vocabulary Word Search 2 Answer Key

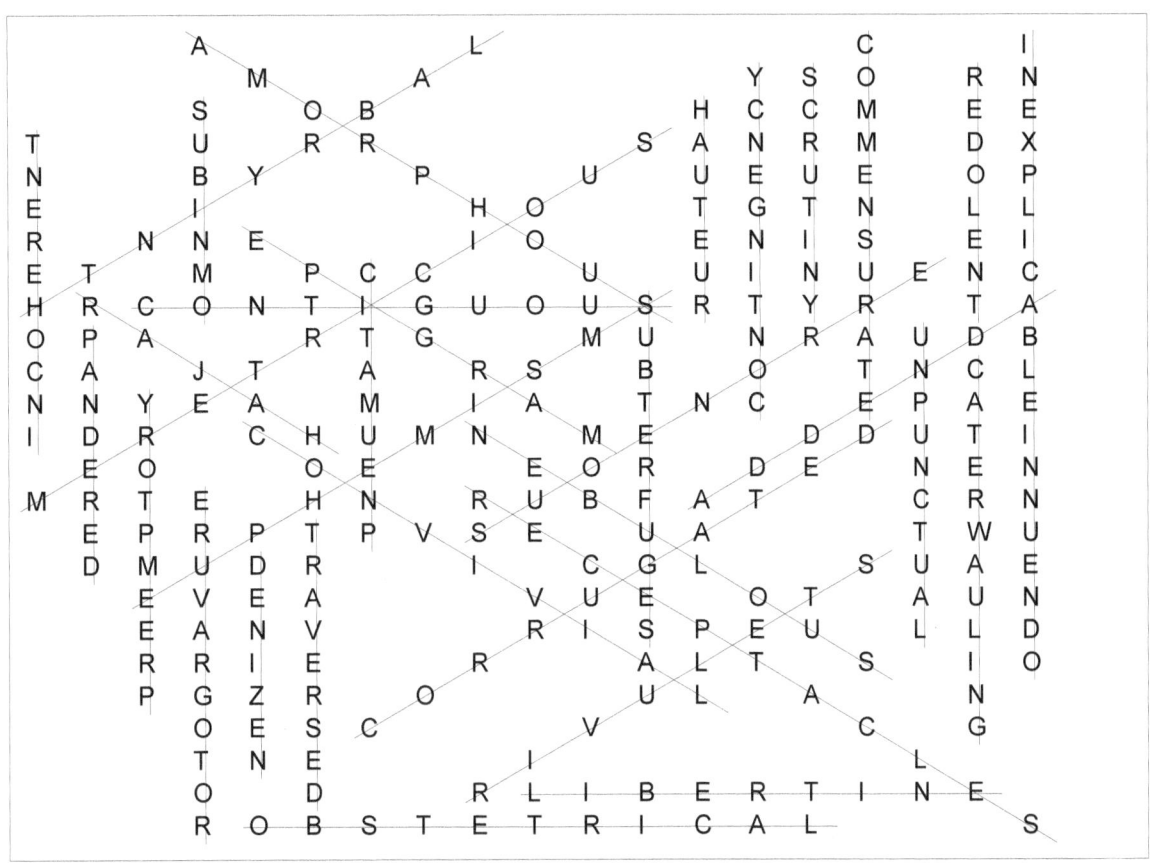

- A container that holds items or matter (11)
- A deceptive stratagem for device (11)
- A long motor vehicle or passengers (7)
- A prince or chief (5)
- A short, witty poem (7)
- A small brook or stream (8)
- Acting or arriving late for the appointed time (10)
- An indirect usually derogatory implication in expression (8)
- An inhabitant (7)
- An intricate structure of interconnecting passages (9)
- Attracting attention in a vulgar manner (12)
- Care of a pregnant woman (11)
- Close observation (8)
- Cloudy, misty or hazy (8)
- Connecting without a break (10)
- Corresponding in size or degree (12)
- Difficult to explain (12)
- Haughtiness in bearing and attitude (7)
- Lacking definite form (9)
- Merry; festive (9)
- Mistaken (9)
- One who acts without moral restraint (9)
- Printed material, such as a newspaper (11)
- Relating to air or other gases (9)
- Shrill, discordant sound (12)
- Something incidental to something else (11)
- Suggestive (8)
- The act of substituting a mild indirect term for a harsh, blunt or offensive one (10)
- Things that are added, esp. a supplement to a book (7)
- To act as a go-between in sexual intrigues (8)
- To shape into folds or parallel ridges and grooves (10)
- To take the place of (10)
- To travel or pass across (9)
- Unable to think in a clear or orderly manner (10)

The Great Gatsby Vocabulary Word Search 3

```
U G T N S U B T E R F U G E S K Z E C Z
B N W M M U K E N N R B F M M Q X T A H
J X P Q D R P M U X P F D E C P H A R V
L L Q U V N W E Q P L B L M O R T R A Y
L A I C N I V O R P H B P S S N Q O V P
Y P V B C C M P D C A E T T E P F B A V
I K R Z E T T C R C I U M R R K F O N T
C N N E S R K U I E L L E I L X Q R S C
K O N N C J T L A A E H I C S L V R A Z
C E M U M E P I T L O M S O X M W O R K
A X D M E X P I N C R C P N U G S C Y S
T T K P E N O T N E E N P T L S B A X B
E E C N Y N D I A G D W R I O T V D J X
R M I E N L S O X C O J P G R R P D L V
W P J U I G Z U N X L B J U H V Y E Z W
A O H M T P T P R Y E E D O X P D N R C
U R L A U P P R V A N E S U C D G D H L
L I A T R I V U L E T S D S E W R A A P
I Z B I C S S K B A M E U S X V U I A W
N I R C S U Q N G A T O R H F T V N B Z
G N Y C B X Y U R X L E H Q E I D W Y M
L G I I D C R G G U V A G U V E Z R D N
P N N Q L R I H B A J B R N R S D W R G
N M T J O P B E R A S U O E N O R R E G
O G H C E T N T R T K C D E N I Z E N W
```

ADDENDA	EPIGRAM	LABRYINTH	RECEPTACLES
CARAVANSARY	ERRONEOUS	LIBERTINE	REDOLENT
CATERWAULING	EUPHEMISMS	NEBULOUS	RIVULETS
COMMENSURATE	EXPOSTULATION	OMNIBUS	SCRUTINY
CONTIGUOUS	EXTEMPORIZING	PANDERED	SUBTERFUGES
CONVIVIAL	HAUTEUR	PNEUMATIC	SUPERCILIOUS
CORROBORATE	INCOHERENT	PREEMPTORY	TRAVERSED
CORRUGATED	INEXPLICABLE	PROVINCIAL	UNPUNCTUAL
DENIZEN	INNUENDO	RAJAH	

The Great Gatsby Vocabulary Word Search 3 Answer Key

ADDENDA	EPIGRAM	LABRYINTH	RECEPTACLES
CARAVANSARY	ERRONEOUS	LIBERTINE	REDOLENT
CATERWAULING	EUPHEMISMS	NEBULOUS	RIVULETS
COMMENSURATE	EXPOSTULATION	OMNIBUS	SCRUTINY
CONTIGUOUS	EXTEMPORIZING	PANDERED	SUBTERFUGES
CONVIVIAL	HAUTEUR	PNEUMATIC	SUPERCILIOUS
CORROBORATE	INCOHERENT	PREEMPTORY	TRAVERSED
CORRUGATED	INEXPLICABLE	PROVINCIAL	UNPUNCTUAL
DENIZEN	INNUENDO	RAJAH	

The Great Gatsby Vocabulary Word Search 4

```
P Z K Z S C S L S W P T R R D J D B L N
G N V C O R R O B O R A T E E B L H Z B
J K E Y R O T P M E E R P J R P I H J Z
D G R U C P J L Y N H L Z H E M B T C N
G C O M M E N S U R A T E A D D E N D A
N S T Z L A A N C I H M V L N G R I S K
C I O S G J T M V R L K B Z A Y T Y T L
X N G S U T J I O A U S S U P T I R E S
Y E R G J B V R C R U T N S L R N B L F
D X A Y C N T I U O P O I A S A E A U B
E P V W O A R E I E I H U N B V T L V C
N L U C E T T C R T P T O K Y E C O I Y
I I R Z E U I E A F C I T U X R A G R N
Z C E T A R P L R N U N G J S S R H E Y
E A S H T N U H U W E G J R H E A T C X
N B J E R T E P E L A S E S A D V L E F
O L R V S A N B O M U U U S Z M A B P V
S E Z O P U J D U B I O L F N I N J T F
M F P H B W E A I L E S G I C F S B A V
W X B K T R J N H N O W M N N X A L C C
E R X Q P T M S O S Y U I S T G R D L X
L Q Z F L O S R J G T V S X G M Y M E S
V F X G K Y R G S U O U G I T N O C S K
D T B W L E C O R R U G A T E D G L R P
I N N U E N D O P I N C O H E R E N T H
```

ADDENDA	EPIGRAM	MERETRICIOUS	REDOLENT
AMORPHOUS	ERRONEOUS	NEBULOUS	RIVULETS
CARAVANSARY	EUPHEMISMS	OBSTETRICAL	ROTOGRAVURE
CATERWAULING	EXPOSTULATION	OMNIBUS	SCRUTINY
COMMENSURATE	HAUTEUR	PANDERED	SOMNAMBULATORY
CONTIGUOUS	INCOHERENT	PNEUMATIC	SUBTERFUGES
CONVIVIAL	INEXPLICABLE	PREEMPTORY	TRAVERSED
CORROBORATE	INNUENDO	PROVINCIAL	UNPUNCTUAL
CORRUGATED	LABRYINTH	RAJAH	
DENIZEN	LIBERTINE	RECEPTACLES	

The Great Gatsby Vocabulary Word Search 4 Answer Key

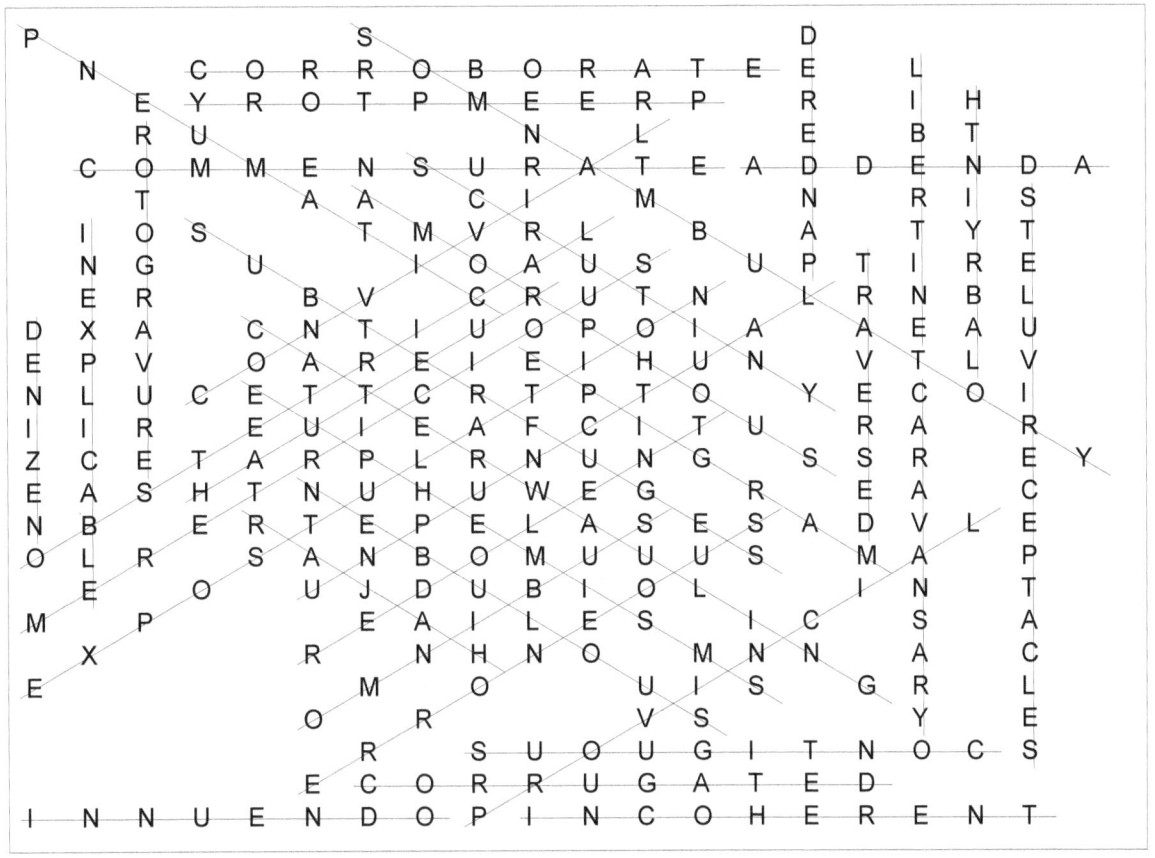

ADDENDA	EPIGRAM	MERETRICIOUS	REDOLENT
AMORPHOUS	ERRONEOUS	NEBULOUS	RIVULETS
CARAVANSARY	EUPHEMISMS	OBSTETRICAL	ROTOGRAVURE
CATERWAULING	EXPOSTULATION	OMNIBUS	SCRUTINY
COMMENSURATE	HAUTEUR	PANDERED	SOMNAMBULATORY
CONTIGUOUS	INCOHERENT	PNEUMATIC	SUBTERFUGES
CONVIVIAL	INEXPLICABLE	PREEMPTORY	TRAVERSED
CORROBORATE	INNUENDO	PROVINCIAL	UNPUNCTUAL
CORRUGATED	LABRYINTH	RAJAH	
DENIZEN	LIBERTINE	RECEPTACLES	

The Great Gatsby Vocabulary Crossword 1

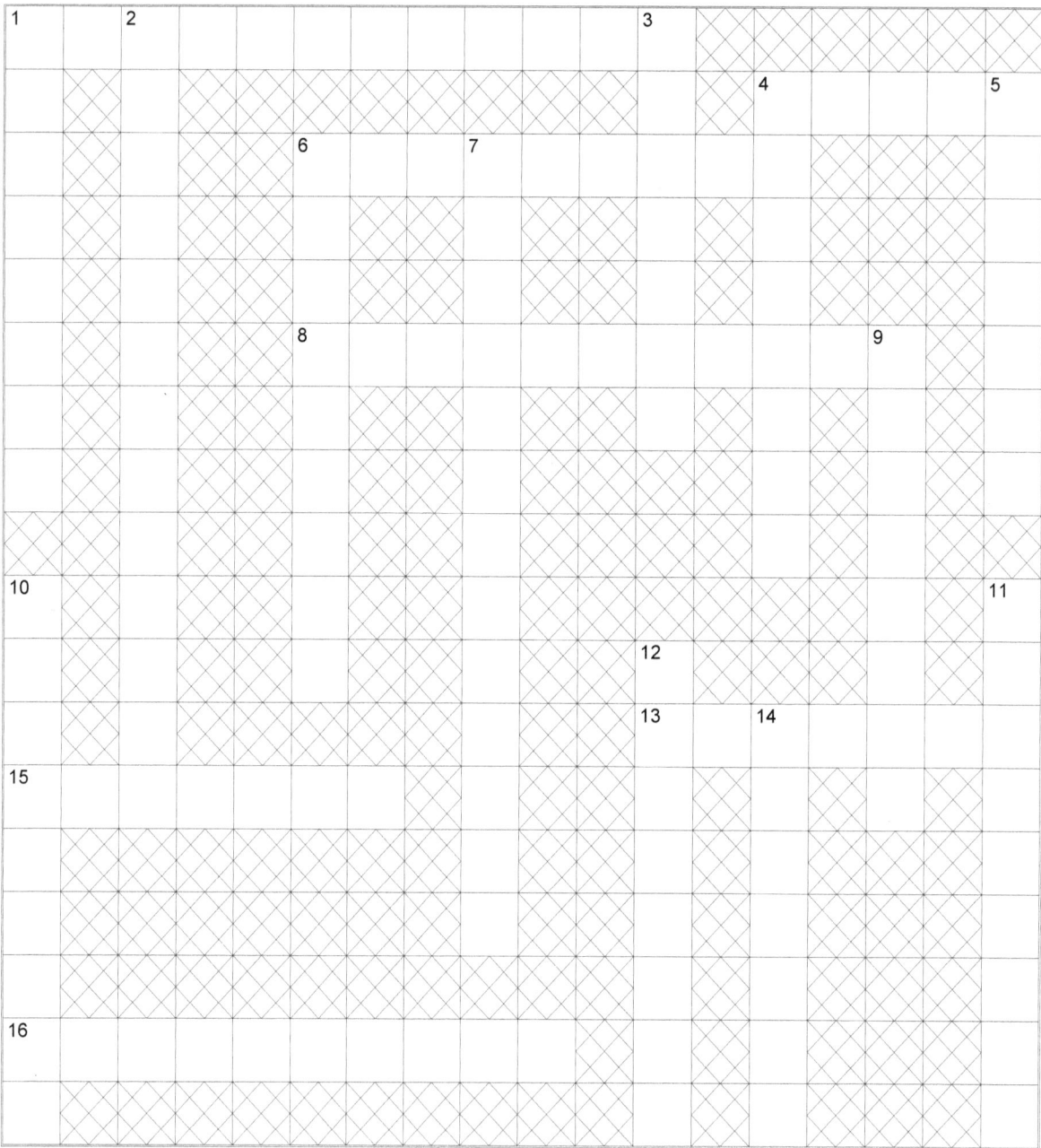

Across
1. Difficult to explain
4. A prince or chief
6. One who acts without moral restraint
8. A container that holds items or matter
13. Things that are added, esp. a supplement to a book
15. A long motor vehicle for passengers
16. Acting or arriving late for the appointed time

5. Haughtiness in bearing and attitude
6. An intricate structure of interconnecting passages
7. To perform without prior preparation
9. Close observation
10. Mistaken
11. To travel or pass across
12. To act as a go-between in sexual intrigues
14. An inhabitant

Down
1. An indirect usually derogatory implication in expression
2. To dissuade or correct
3. A short, witty poem
4. Suggestive

The Great Gatsby Vocabulary Crossword 1 Answer Key

	1 I	N	2 E	X	P	L	I	C	A	B	3 L E	E		4 R	A	J	A	5 H

(Filled grid with answers)

Across
1. Difficult to explain
4. A prince or chief
6. One who acts without moral restraint
8. A container that holds items or matter
13. Things that are added, esp. a supplement to a book
15. A long motor vehicle for passengers
16. Acting or arriving late for the appointed time

Down
1. An indirect usually derogatory implication in expression
2. To dissuade or correct
3. A short, witty poem
4. Suggestive
5. Haughtiness in bearing and attitude
6. An intricate structure of interconnecting passages
7. To perform without prior preparation
9. Close observation
10. Mistaken
11. To travel or pass across
12. To act as a go-between in sexual intrigues
14. An inhabitant

The Great Gatsby Vocabulary Crossword 2

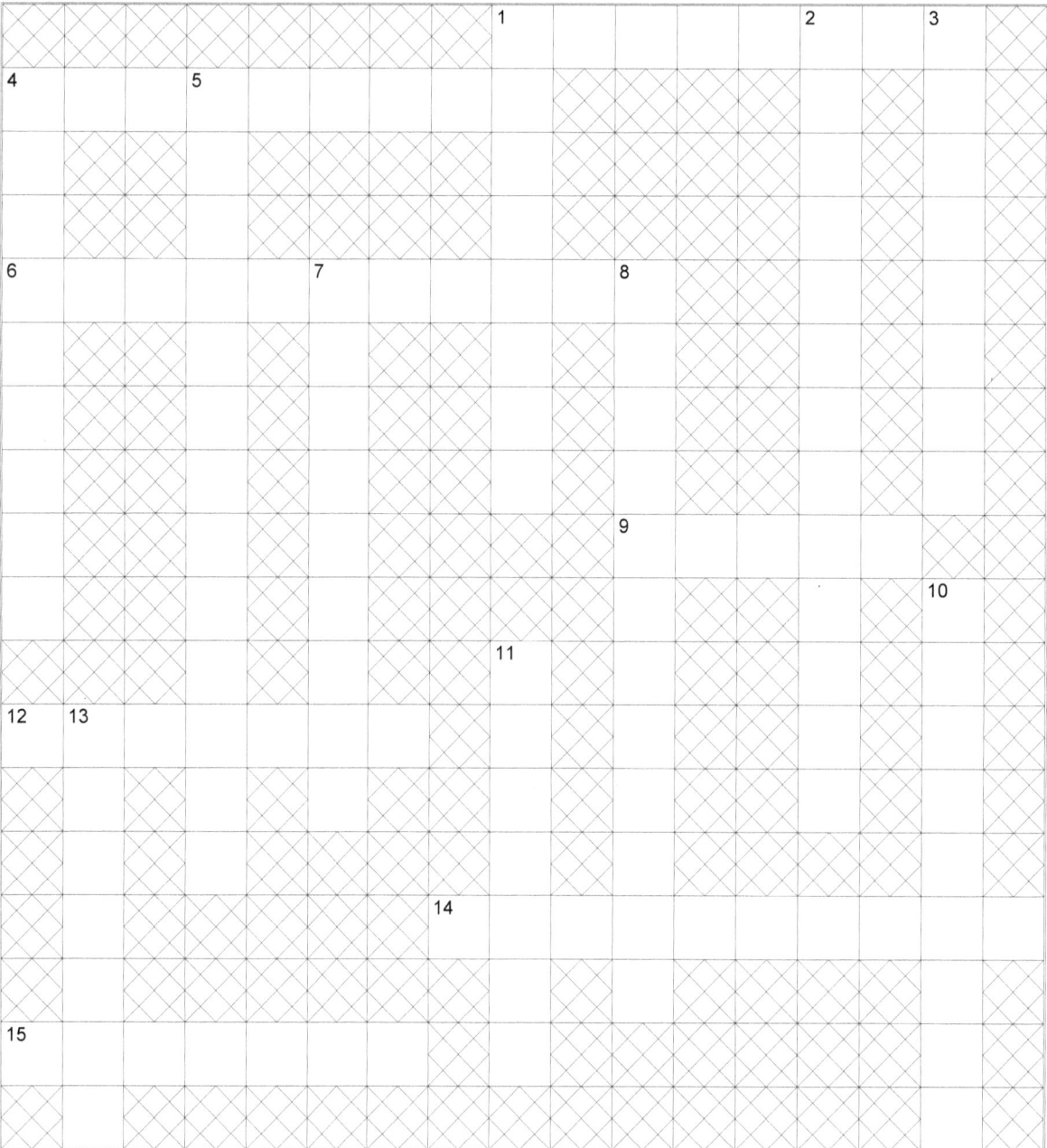

Across
1. A small brook or stream
4. One who acts without moral restraint
6. A container that holds items or matter
9. A prince or chief
12. An inhabitant
14. Acting or arriving late for the appointed time
15. Haughtiness in bearing and attitude

Down
1. Suggestive
2. To dissuade or correct
3. Close observation
4. An intricate structure of interconnecting passages
5. To perform without prior preparation
7. To travel or pass across
8. Feeling or showing haughty disdain
10. Relating to air or other gases
11. Things that are added, esp. a supplement to a book
13. A short, witty poem

The Great Gatsby Vocabulary Crossword 2 Answer Key

							¹R	I	V	U	L	²E	T	³S	
⁴L	I	B	⁵E	R	T	I	N	E				X		C	
A			X				D					P		R	
B			T				O					O		U	
⁶R	E	C	E	P	⁷T	A	C	L	E	⁸S		S		T	
Y			M		R		E			U		T		I	
I			P		A		N			P		U		N	
N			O		V		T			E		L		Y	
T			R		E					⁹R	A	J	A	H	
H			I		R					C		T		¹⁰P	
			Z		S			¹¹A		I		I		N	
¹²D	¹³E	N	I	Z	E	N		D		L		O		E	
	P		N		D			D		I		N		U	
	I		G					E		O				M	
	G						¹⁴U	N	P	U	N	C	T	U	A	L
	R						D		S					T	
¹⁵H	A	U	T	E	U	R	A							I	
	M													C	

Across
1. A small brook or stream
4. One who acts without moral restraint
6. A container that holds items or matter
9. A prince or chief
12. An inhabitant
14. Acting or arriving late for the appointed time
15. Haughtiness in bearing and attitude

Down
1. Suggestive
2. To dissuade or correct
3. Close observation
4. An intricate structure of interconnecting passages
5. To perform without prior preparation
7. To travel or pass across
8. Feeling or showing haughty disdain
10. Relating to air or other gases
11. Things that are added, esp. a supplement to a book
13. A short, witty poem

The Great Gatsby Vocabulary Crossword 3

Across
1. A show, pretense or display
5. Things that are added, esp. a supplement to a book
6. A prince or chief
8. One who acts without moral restraint
12. A container that holds items or matter
14. A short, witty poem
16. An inhabitant
17. Care of a pregnant woman

Down
2. Merry; festive
3. A long motor vehicle for passengers
4. Close observation
7. Lacking definite form
8. An intricate structure of interconnecting passages
9. To perform without prior preparation
10. Difficult to explain
11. Acting or arriving late for the appointed time
13. Suggestive
15. A small brook or stream

The Great Gatsby Vocabulary Crossword 3 Answer Key

```
      A F F E C T A T I O N S
              O         M   C
        A D D E N D A   N   R A J A H
              V         I   U       M
    L I B E R T I N E       B   T   O
    A       X   V       I   U   I   R   U
    B       T   I       N   S   N   P   N
    R E C E P T A C L E S       Y   H   P
    Y       M   L       X           O   U
    I       P   R   E P I G R A M   U   N
    N       O   E   L       I       S   C
    T       R   D   I       V           T
    H       I   O   C       U           U
            Z   L   A       L           A
    D E N I Z E N   O B S T E T R I C A L
            N   N   L       T
            G   T   E       S
```

Across
1. A show, pretense or display
5. Things that are added, esp. a supplement to a book
6. A prince or chief
8. One who acts without moral restraint
12. A container that holds items or matter
14. A short, witty poem
16. An inhabitant
17. Care of a pregnant woman

Down
2. Merry; festive
3. A long motor vehicle for passengers
4. Close observation
7. Lacking definite form
8. An intricate structure of interconnecting passages
9. To perform without prior preparation
10. Difficult to explain
11. Acting or arriving late for the appointed time
13. Suggestive
15. A small brook or stream

The Great Gatsby Vocabulary Crossword 4

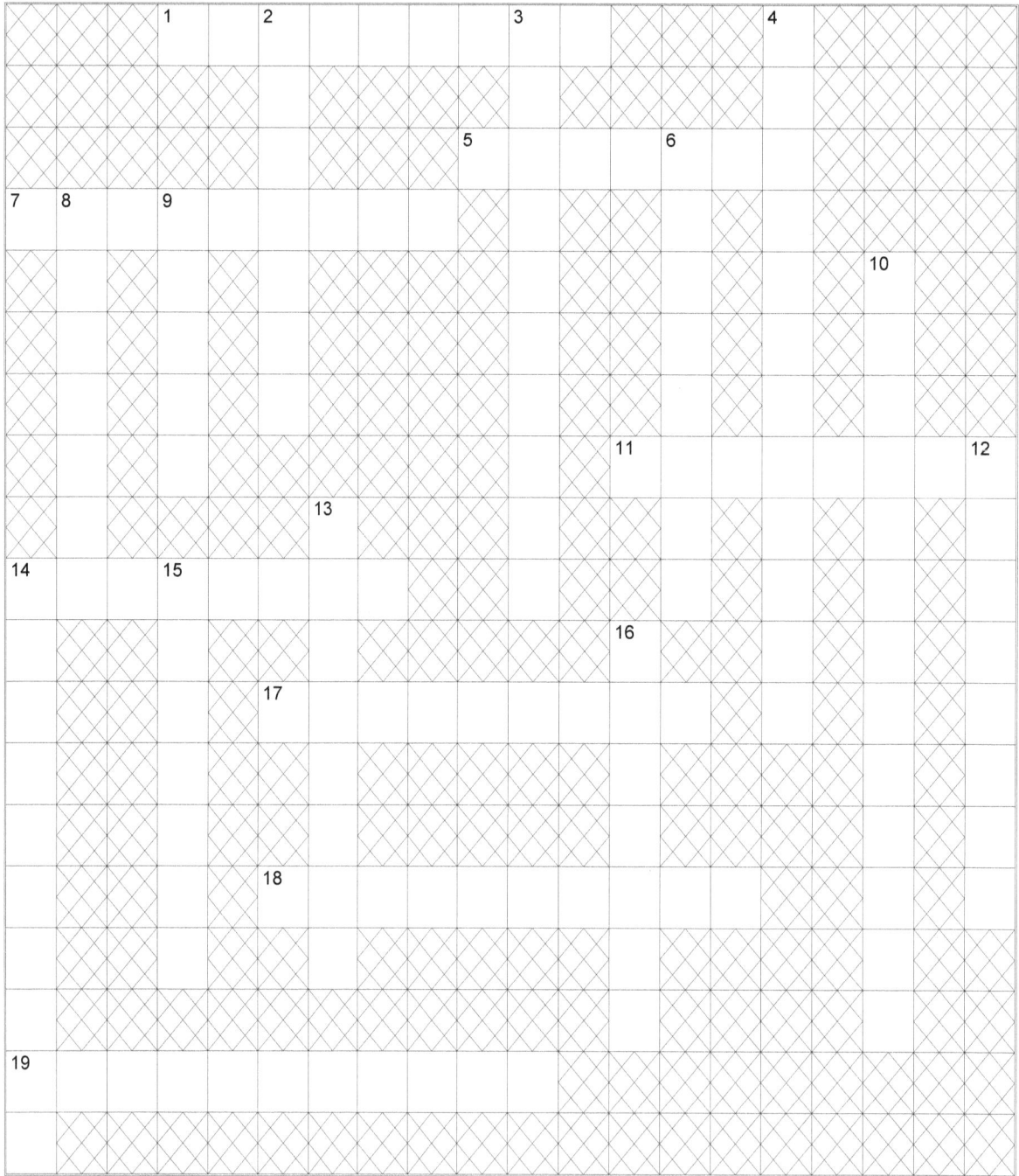

Across
1. Lacking definite form
5. A short, witty poem
7. An intricate structure of interconnecting passages
11. Cloudy, misty or hazy
14. To act as a go-between in sexual intrigues
17. Merry; festive
18. Unable to think in a clear or orderly manner
19. A container that holds items or matter

Down
2. A long motor vehicle for passengers
3. Acting or arriving late for the appointed time
4. Corresponding in size or degree
6. A small brook or stream
8. Things that are added, esp. a supplement to a book
9. A prince or chief
10. To dissuade or correct
12. Close observation
13. Suggestive
14. To take the place of
15. An inhabitant
16. Haughtiness in bearing and attitude

The Great Gatsby Vocabulary Crossword 4 Answer Key

Across
1. Lacking definite form
5. A short, witty poem
7. An intricate structure of interconnecting passages
11. Cloudy, misty or hazy
14. To act as a go-between in sexual intrigues
17. Merry; festive
18. Unable to think in a clear or orderly manner
19. A container that holds items or matter

Down
2. A long motor vehicle for passengers
3. Acting or arriving late for the appointed time
4. Corresponding in size or degree
6. A small brook or stream
8. Things that are added, esp. a supplement to a book
9. A prince or chief
10. To dissuade or correct
12. Close observation
13. Suggestive
14. To take the place of
15. An inhabitant
16. Haughtiness in bearing and attitude

The Great Gatsby Vocabulary Juggle Letters 1

1. SXTNUTIPAOOLE = 1. _____
   To dissuade or correct

2. TICYNGONNCE = 2. _____
   Something incidental to something else

3. NILLEXPIBAEC = 3. _____
   Difficult to explain

4. NIRAGLACTUWE = 4. _____
   Shrill, discordant sound

5. ENSOLBUU = 5. _____
   Cloudy, misty or hazy

6. OURPSAMOH = 6. _____
   Lacking definite form

7. LESTBORTIAC = 7. _____
   Care of a pregnant woman

8. OCINLVVAI = 8. _____
   Merry; festive

9. CAELRSPECET = 9. _____
   A container that holds items or matter

10. RVRAEOUTRGO = 10. _____
    Printed material, such as a newspaper

11. INUMBSO = 11. _____
    A long motor vehicle for passengers

12. NRELIITBE = 12. _____
    One who acts without moral restraint

13. HRJAA = 13. _____
    A prince or chief

14. AMIUEPTNC = 14. _____
    Relating to air or other gases

15. SMRCUOEENTAM = 15. _____
    Corresponding in size or degree

The Great Gatsby Vocabulary Juggle Letters 1 Answer Key

1. SXTNUTIPAOOLE = 1. EXPOSTULATION
   To dissuade or correct

2. TICYNGONNCE = 2. CONTINGENCY
   Something incidental to something else

3. NILLEXPIBAEC = 3. INEXPLICABLE
   Difficult to explain

4. NIRAGLACTUWE = 4. CATERWAULING
   Shrill, discordant sound

5. ENSOLBUU = 5. NEBULOUS
   Cloudy, misty or hazy

6. OURPSAMOH = 6. AMORPHOUS
   Lacking definite form

7. LESTBORTIAC = 7. OBSTETRICAL
   Care of a pregnant woman

8. OCINLVVAI = 8. CONVIVIAL
   Merry; festive

9. CAELRSPECET = 9. RECEPTACLES
   A container that holds items or matter

10. RVRAEOUTRGO = 10. ROTOGRAVURE
    Printed material, such as a newspaper

11. INUMBSO = 11. OMNIBUS
    A long motor vehicle for passengers

12. NRELIITBE = 12. LIBERTINE
    One who acts without moral restraint

13. HRJAA = 13. RAJAH
    A prince or chief

14. AMIUEPTNC = 14. PNEUMATIC
    Relating to air or other gases

15. SMRCUOEENTAM = 15. COMMENSURATE
    Corresponding in size or degree

The Great Gatsby Vocabulary Juggle Letters 2

1. NTAETXOSUPLOI   = 1. _____
   To dissuade or correct

2. OCTSGUNIOU   = 2. _____
   Connecting without a break

3. RARDGTUEOC   = 3. _____
   To shape into folds or parallel ridges and grooves

4. IBESCTLTRAO   = 4. _____
   Care of a pregnant woman

5. OSRUOPHAM   = 5. _____
   Lacking definite form

6. RTPIIEZGNEXMO   = 6. _____
   To perform without prior preparation

7. EUHUTAR   = 7. _____
   Haughtiness in bearing and attitude

8. EAAOINFFTTSC   = 8. _____
   A show, pretense or display

9. USEBUFTESGR   = 9. _____
   A deceptive stratagem or device

10. CIOAVIRNLP   =10. _____
    Limited in perspective

11. TUROGERRAOV   =11. _____
    Printed material, such as a newspaper

12. ERUNOSREO   =12. _____
    Mistaken

13. INEZNED   =13. _____
    An inhabitant

14. USMNBIO   =14. _____
    A long motor vehicle for passengers

15. UUNEOBLS   =15. _____
    Cloudy, misty or hazy

The Great Gatsby Vocabulary Juggle Letters 2 Answer Key

1. NTAETXOSUPLOI = 1. EXPOSTULATION
   To dissuade or correct

2. OCTSGUNIOU = 2. CONTIGUOUS
   Connecting without a break

3. RARDGTUEOC = 3. CORRUGATED
   To shape into folds or parallel ridges and grooves

4. IBESCTLTRAO = 4. OBSTETRICAL
   Care of a pregnant woman

5. OSRUOPHAM = 5. AMORPHOUS
   Lacking definite form

6. RTPIIEZGNEXMO = 6. EXTEMPORIZING
   To perform without prior preparation

7. EUHUTAR = 7. HAUTEUR
   Haughtiness in bearing and attitude

8. EAAOINFFTTSC = 8. AFFECTATIONS
   A show, pretense or display

9. USEBUFTESGR = 9. SUBTERFUGES
   A deceptive stratagem or device

10. CIOAVIRNLP = 10. PROVINCIAL
    Limited in perspective

11. TUROGERRAOV = 11. ROTOGRAVURE
    Printed material, such as a newspaper

12. ERUNOSREO = 12. ERRONEOUS
    Mistaken

13. INEZNED = 13. DENIZEN
    An inhabitant

14. USMNBIO = 14. OMNIBUS
    A long motor vehicle for passengers

15. UUNEOBLS = 15. NEBULOUS
    Cloudy, misty or hazy

The Great Gatsby Vocabulary Juggle Letters 3

1. OOUUNGTSCI = 1. _____
   Connecting without a break

2. OETELRND = 2. _____
   Suggestive

3. AVINLCOVI = 3. _____
   Merry; festive

4. IMNUSBO = 4. _____
   A long motor vehicle for passengers

5. MRAIEGP = 5. _____
   A short, witty poem

6. EGSRFTEUSBU = 6. _____
   A deceptive stratagem or device

7. YECGNCOTNIN = 7. _____
   Something incidental to something else

8. BRNIALTYH = 8. _____
   An intricate structure of interconnecting passages

9. MHPMSEUSEI = 9. _____
   The act of substituting a mild indirect term for a harsh, blunt or offensive one

10. MOYRTPRPEE =10. _____
    To take the place of

11. SBOUUENL =11. _____
    Cloudy, misty or hazy

12. MSCNOETRMUEA =12. _____
    Corresponding in size or degree

13. ZINOMGXPETERI =13. _____
    To perform without prior preparation

14. ZNENIED =14. _____
    An inhabitant

15. BEITENRLI =15. _____
    One who acts without moral restraint

The Great Gatsby Vocabulary Jugle Letters 3 Answer Key

1. OOUUNGTSCI = 1. CONTIGUOUS
   Connecting without a break

2. OETELRND = 2. REDOLENT
   Suggestive

3. AVINLCOVI = 3. CONVIVIAL
   Merry; festive

4. IMNUSBO = 4. OMNIBUS
   A long motor vehicle for passengers

5. MRAIEGP = 5. EPIGRAM
   A short, witty poem

6. EGSRFTEUSBU = 6. SUBTERFUGES
   A deceptive stratagem or device

7. YECGNCOTNIN = 7. CONTINGENCY
   Something incidental to something else

8. BRNIALTYH = 8. LABRYINTH
   An intricate structure of interconnecting passages

9. MHPMSEUSEI = 9. EUPHEMISMS
   The act of substituting a mild indirect term for a harsh, blunt or offensive one

10. MOYRTPRPEE =10. PREEMPTORY
    To take the place of

11. SBOUUENL =11. NEBULOUS
    Cloudy, misty or hazy

12. MSCNOETRMUEA =12. COMMENSURATE
    Corresponding in size or degree

13. ZINOMGXPETERI =13. EXTEMPORIZING
    To perform without prior preparation

14. ZNENIED =14. DENIZEN
    An inhabitant

15. BEITENRLI =15. LIBERTINE
    One who acts without moral restraint

The Great Gatsby Vocabulary Juggle Letters 4

1. RDNDPEAE = 1. _____
   To act as a go-between in sexual intrigues

2. RIAPEGM = 2. _____
   A short, witty poem

3. VIVNOLIAC = 3. _____
   Merry; festive

4. NZNEDIE = 4. _____
   An inhabitant

5. STTECAIOFFNA = 5. _____
   A show, pretense or display

6. UCGSTOIONU = 6. _____
   Connecting without a break

7. LMSMTONBAYOURA = 7. _____
   To walk in a sleeplike condition

8. ACTERLSIBTO = 8. _____
   Care of a pregnant woman

9. AUCNUNULTP = 9. _____
   Acting or arriving late for the appointed time

10. SNUOREEOR =10. _____
    Mistaken

11. EUBRUETFSSG =11. _____
    A deceptive stratagem or device

12. ERVRGUTOARO =12. _____
    Printed material, such as a newspaper

13. LISETAOOUPXTN =13. _____
    To dissuade or correct

14. TRLNGEUWAICA =14. _____
    Shrill, discordant sound

15. EOEMRPTRYP =15. _____
    To take the place of

The Great Gatsby Vocabulary Juggle Leters 4 Answer Key

1. RDNDPEAE = 1. PANDERED
   To act as a go-between in sexual intrigues
2. RIAPEGM = 2. EPIGRAM
   A short, witty poem
3. VIVNOLIAC = 3. CONVIVIAL
   Merry; festive
4. NZNEDIE = 4. DENIZEN
   An inhabitant
5. STTECAIOFFNA = 5. AFFECTATIONS
   A show, pretense or display
6. UCGSTOIONU = 6. CONTIGUOUS
   Connecting without a break
7. LMSMTONBAYOURA = 7. SOMNAMBULATORY
   To walk in a sleeplike condition
8. ACTERLSIBTO = 8. OBSTETRICAL
   Care of a pregnant woman
9. AUCNUNULTP = 9. UNPUNCTUAL
   Acting or arriving late for the appointed time
10. SNUOREEOR =10. ERRONEOUS
    Mistaken
11. EUBRUETFSSG =11. SUBTERFUGES
    A deceptive stratagem or device
12. ERVRGUTOARO =12. ROTOGRAVURE
    Printed material, such as a newspaper
13. LISETAOOUPXTN =13. EXPOSTULATION
    To dissuade or correct
14. TRLNGEUWAICA =14. CATERWAULING
    Shrill, discordant sound
15. EOEMRPTRYP =15. PREEMPTORY
    To take the place of

Copyrighted

ADDENDA	Things that are added, esp. a supplement to a book
AFFECTATIONS	A show, pretense or display
AMORPHOUS	Lacking definite form
CARAVANSARY	A large inn
CATERWAULING	Shrill, discordant sound
COMMENSURATE	Corresponding in size or degree

CONTIGUOUS	Connecting without a break
CONTINGENCY	Something incidental to something else
CONVIVIAL	Merry; festive
CORROBORATE	To strengthen or support with other evidence
CORRUGATED	To shape into folds or parallel ridges and grooves
DENIZEN	An inhabitant

EPIGRAM	A short, witty poem
ERRONEOUS	Mistaken
EUPHEMISMS	The act of substituting a mild indirect term for a harsh, blunt or offensive one
EXPOSTULATION	To dissuade or correct
EXTEMPORIZING	To perform without prior preparation
HAUTEUR	Haughtiness in bearing and attitude

INCOHERENT	Unable to think in a clear or orderly manner
INEXPLICABLE	Difficult to explain
INNUENDO	An indirect usually derogatory implication in expression
LABRYINTH	An intricate structure of interconnecting passages
LIBERTINE	One who acts without moral restraint
MERETRICIOUS	Attracting attention in a vulgar manner

NEBULOUS	Cloudy, misty or hazy
OBSTETRICAL	Care of a pregnant woman
OMNIBUS	A long motor vehicle for passengers
PANDERED	To act as a go-between in sexual intrigues
PNEUMATIC	Relating to air or other gases
PREEMPTORY	To take the place of

PROVINCIAL	Limited in perspective
RAJAH	A prince or chief
RECEPTACLES	A container that holds items or matter
REDOLENT	Suggestive
RIVULETS	A small brook or stream
ROTOGRAVURE	Printed material, such as a newspaper

SCRUTINY	Close observation
SOMNAMBULATORY	To walk in a sleeplike condition
SUBTERFUGES	A deceptive stratagem or device
SUPERCILIOUS	Feeling or showing haughty disdain
TRAVERSED	To travel or pass across
UNPUNCTUAL	Acting or arriving late for the appointed time

The Great Gatsby Vocabulary

PREEMPTORY	INCOHERENT	AMORPHOUS	RIVULETS	ERRONEOUS
CONTINGENCY	CONTIGUOUS	REDOLENT	LIBERTINE	SUPERCILIOUS
LABRYINTH	EXPOSTULATION	FREE SPACE	RECEPTACLES	SOMNAMBULATORY
EUPHEMISMS	TRAVERSED	PANDERED	CATERWAULING	CORROBORATE
NEBULOUS	DENIZEN	INNUENDO	RAJAH	OMNIBUS

The Great Gatsby Vocabulary

OBSTETRICAL	EPIGRAM	ADDENDA	CONVIVIAL	SUBTERFUGES
MERETRICIOUS	COMMENSURATE	PNEUMATIC	CARAVANSARY	HAUTEUR
UNPUNCTUAL	CORRUGATED	FREE SPACE	ROTOGRAVURE	SCRUTINY
INEXPLICABLE	EXTEMPORIZING	OMNIBUS	RAJAH	INNUENDO
DENIZEN	NEBULOUS	CORROBORATE	CATERWAULING	PANDERED

The Great Gatsby Vocabulary

NEBULOUS	CATERWAULING	OMNIBUS	TRAVERSED	CORROBORATE
PANDERED	MERETRICIOUS	SCRUTINY	CARAVANSARY	ADDENDA
CONTINGENCY	LABRYINTH	FREE SPACE	UNPUNCTUAL	CONVIVIAL
RECEPTACLES	EUPHEMISMS	CORRUGATED	RIVULETS	SOMNAMBULATORY
CONTIGUOUS	ROTOGRAVURE	DENIZEN	AMORPHOUS	INEXPLICABLE

The Great Gatsby Vocabulary

EXTEMPORIZING	INNUENDO	OBSTETRICAL	ERRONEOUS	SUPERCILIOUS
AFFECTATIONS	PREEMPTORY	INCOHERENT	RAJAH	PNEUMATIC
REDOLENT	COMMENSURATE	FREE SPACE	SUBTERFUGES	HAUTEUR
PROVINCIAL	EPIGRAM	INEXPLICABLE	AMORPHOUS	DENIZEN
ROTOGRAVURE	CONTIGUOUS	SOMNAMBULATORY	RIVULETS	CORRUGATED

The Great Gatsby Vocabulary

COMMENSURATE	CONVIVIAL	PANDERED	EXTEMPORIZING	OMNIBUS
AMORPHOUS	SUPERCILIOUS	EUPHEMISMS	OBSTETRICAL	CONTINGENCY
SCRUTINY	CARAVANSARY	FREE SPACE	INEXPLICABLE	EPIGRAM
LABRYINTH	DENIZEN	RAJAH	EXPOSTULATION	CONTIGUOUS
HAUTEUR	MERETRICIOUS	REDOLENT	UNPUNCTUAL	INCOHERENT

The Great Gatsby Vocabulary

CORROBORATE	INNUENDO	CATERWAULING	NEBULOUS	ROTOGRAVURE
ADDENDA	RECEPTACLES	PNEUMATIC	PREEMPTORY	CORRUGATED
RIVULETS	PROVINCIAL	FREE SPACE	TRAVERSED	AFFECTATIONS
ERRONEOUS	LIBERTINE	INCOHERENT	UNPUNCTUAL	REDOLENT
MERETRICIOUS	HAUTEUR	CONTIGUOUS	EXPOSTULATION	RAJAH

The Great Gatsby Vocabulary

CONTINGENCY	ADDENDA	RIVULETS	CATERWAULING	EXPOSTULATION
RAJAH	TRAVERSED	UNPUNCTUAL	HAUTEUR	AFFECTATIONS
INNUENDO	CONTIGUOUS	FREE SPACE	SUPERCILIOUS	CARAVANSARY
RECEPTACLES	LIBERTINE	NEBULOUS	PROVINCIAL	CORROBORATE
ERRONEOUS	EPIGRAM	PREEMPTORY	EXTEMPORIZING	CONVIVIAL

The Great Gatsby Vocabulary

INEXPLICABLE	ROTOGRAVURE	SOMNAMBULATORY	DENIZEN	OBSTETRICAL
OMNIBUS	AMORPHOUS	LABRYINTH	REDOLENT	EUPHEMISMS
CORRUGATED	SUBTERFUGES	FREE SPACE	PANDERED	PNEUMATIC
INCOHERENT	SCRUTINY	CONVIVIAL	EXTEMPORIZING	PREEMPTORY
EPIGRAM	ERRONEOUS	CORROBORATE	PROVINCIAL	NEBULOUS

The Great Gatsby Vocabulary

SOMNAMBULATORY	COMMENSURATE	AMORPHOUS	CONTINGENCY	INCOHERENT
CORROBORATE	PNEUMATIC	MERETRICIOUS	EXTEMPORIZING	PANDERED
CARAVANSARY	SUBTERFUGES	FREE SPACE	AFFECTATIONS	SCRUTINY
NEBULOUS	SUPERCILIOUS	RECEPTACLES	INNUENDO	EXPOSTULATION
PREEMPTORY	CORRUGATED	CONTIGUOUS	DENIZEN	LABRYINTH

The Great Gatsby Vocabulary

LIBERTINE	CONVIVIAL	OBSTETRICAL	OMNIBUS	ROTOGRAVURE
EPIGRAM	TRAVERSED	INEXPLICABLE	ERRONEOUS	RAJAH
CATERWAULING	PROVINCIAL	FREE SPACE	RIVULETS	UNPUNCTUAL
ADDENDA	REDOLENT	LABRYINTH	DENIZEN	CONTIGUOUS
CORRUGATED	PREEMPTORY	EXPOSTULATION	INNUENDO	RECEPTACLES

The Great Gatsby Vocabulary

SUBTERFUGES	SUPERCILIOUS	COMMENSURATE	HAUTEUR	EUPHEMISMS
OMNIBUS	DENIZEN	MERETRICIOUS	PANDERED	INNUENDO
REDOLENT	EPIGRAM	FREE SPACE	CATERWAULING	PROVINCIAL
CONTIGUOUS	AMORPHOUS	INEXPLICABLE	ADDENDA	RIVULETS
ROTOGRAVURE	SOMNAMBULATORY	OBSTETRICAL	CONTINGENCY	EXPOSTULATION

The Great Gatsby Vocabulary

EXTEMPORIZING	CARAVANSARY	SCRUTINY	CORRUGATED	PNEUMATIC
NEBULOUS	TRAVERSED	LABRYINTH	AFFECTATIONS	INCOHERENT
CONVIVIAL	UNPUNCTUAL	FREE SPACE	ERRONEOUS	LIBERTINE
RECEPTACLES	CORROBORATE	EXPOSTULATION	CONTINGENCY	OBSTETRICAL
SOMNAMBULATORY	ROTOGRAVURE	RIVULETS	ADDENDA	INEXPLICABLE

The Great Gatsby Vocabulary

CORRUGATED	SUBTERFUGES	SOMNAMBULATORY	LABRYINTH	INCOHERENT
NEBULOUS	SCRUTINY	HAUTEUR	EXTEMPORIZING	EUPHEMISMS
CATERWAULING	PREEMPTORY	FREE SPACE	ROTOGRAVURE	MERETRICIOUS
SUPERCILIOUS	OBSTETRICAL	UNPUNCTUAL	EXPOSTULATION	AMORPHOUS
OMNIBUS	PANDERED	DENIZEN	CORROBORATE	LIBERTINE

The Great Gatsby Vocabulary

CONVIVIAL	INNUENDO	RAJAH	INEXPLICABLE	PROVINCIAL
PNEUMATIC	CONTINGENCY	AFFECTATIONS	RIVULETS	COMMENSURATE
REDOLENT	CONTIGUOUS	FREE SPACE	CARAVANSARY	ERRONEOUS
ADDENDA	EPIGRAM	LIBERTINE	CORROBORATE	DENIZEN
PANDERED	OMNIBUS	AMORPHOUS	EXPOSTULATION	UNPUNCTUAL

The Great Gatsby Vocabulary

LABRYINTH	INEXPLICABLE	EPIGRAM	OBSTETRICAL	RAJAH
PANDERED	NEBULOUS	REDOLENT	CORRUGATED	SOMNAMBULATORY
EUPHEMISMS	TRAVERSED	FREE SPACE	AMORPHOUS	CONVIVIAL
INCOHERENT	HAUTEUR	CONTINGENCY	CONTIGUOUS	COMMENSURATE
LIBERTINE	MERETRICIOUS	SCRUTINY	RIVULETS	OMNIBUS

The Great Gatsby Vocabulary

CATERWAULING	CARAVANSARY	EXTEMPORIZING	RECEPTACLES	ROTOGRAVURE
PROVINCIAL	CORROBORATE	EXPOSTULATION	SUPERCILIOUS	INNUENDO
PREEMPTORY	DENIZEN	FREE SPACE	ADDENDA	UNPUNCTUAL
ERRONEOUS	SUBTERFUGES	OMNIBUS	RIVULETS	SCRUTINY
MERETRICIOUS	LIBERTINE	COMMENSURATE	CONTIGUOUS	CONTINGENCY

The Great Gatsby Vocabulary

INCOHERENT	OBSTETRICAL	OMNIBUS	HAUTEUR	CONTINGENCY
UNPUNCTUAL	LABRYINTH	SCRUTINY	SOMNAMBULATORY	PROVINCIAL
PREEMPTORY	CONTIGUOUS	FREE SPACE	CARAVANSARY	NEBULOUS
PNEUMATIC	EPIGRAM	COMMENSURATE	ADDENDA	INNUENDO
CONVIVIAL	PANDERED	MERETRICIOUS	EUPHEMISMS	CORRUGATED

The Great Gatsby Vocabulary

SUPERCILIOUS	INEXPLICABLE	EXTEMPORIZING	RECEPTACLES	AFFECTATIONS
CORROBORATE	AMORPHOUS	ROTOGRAVURE	EXPOSTULATION	DENIZEN
TRAVERSED	SUBTERFUGES	FREE SPACE	REDOLENT	RIVULETS
LIBERTINE	RAJAH	CORRUGATED	EUPHEMISMS	MERETRICIOUS
PANDERED	CONVIVIAL	INNUENDO	ADDENDA	COMMENSURATE

The Great Gatsby Vocabulary

ADDENDA	LABRYINTH	AFFECTATIONS	OMNIBUS	CATERWAULING
ROTOGRAVURE	PNEUMATIC	PROVINCIAL	RECEPTACLES	CORRUGATED
OBSTETRICAL	COMMENSURATE	FREE SPACE	RAJAH	EUPHEMISMS
TRAVERSED	MERETRICIOUS	CORROBORATE	CONVIVIAL	SUPERCILIOUS
CONTINGENCY	RIVULETS	INEXPLICABLE	EXPOSTULATION	EXTEMPORIZING

The Great Gatsby Vocabulary

INNUENDO	PANDERED	SUBTERFUGES	ERRONEOUS	AMORPHOUS
EPIGRAM	NEBULOUS	INCOHERENT	HAUTEUR	REDOLENT
CONTIGUOUS	UNPUNCTUAL	FREE SPACE	SOMNAMBULATORY	PREEMPTORY
LIBERTINE	CARAVANSARY	EXTEMPORIZING	EXPOSTULATION	INEXPLICABLE
RIVULETS	CONTINGENCY	SUPERCILIOUS	CONVIVIAL	CORROBORATE

The Great Gatsby Vocabulary

UNPUNCTUAL	PROVINCIAL	SUBTERFUGES	LIBERTINE	EPIGRAM
CORROBORATE	PREEMPTORY	CORRUGATED	OMNIBUS	EXTEMPORIZING
CONTIGUOUS	RAJAH	FREE SPACE	DENIZEN	COMMENSURATE
ROTOGRAVURE	LABRYINTH	RIVULETS	RECEPTACLES	HAUTEUR
CARAVANSARY	ADDENDA	SOMNAMBULATORY	AMORPHOUS	INEXPLICABLE

The Great Gatsby Vocabulary

CONTINGENCY	PANDERED	REDOLENT	MERETRICIOUS	CATERWAULING
INCOHERENT	AFFECTATIONS	CONVIVIAL	EUPHEMISMS	PNEUMATIC
ERRONEOUS	INNUENDO	FREE SPACE	SUPERCILIOUS	EXPOSTULATION
NEBULOUS	TRAVERSED	INEXPLICABLE	AMORPHOUS	SOMNAMBULATORY
ADDENDA	CARAVANSARY	HAUTEUR	RECEPTACLES	RIVULETS

The Great Gatsby Vocabulary

ERRONEOUS	CONTIGUOUS	MERETRICIOUS	EXTEMPORIZING	CORRUGATED
SUBTERFUGES	INCOHERENT	ROTOGRAVURE	NEBULOUS	UNPUNCTUAL
PROVINCIAL	RIVULETS	FREE SPACE	AMORPHOUS	OMNIBUS
PANDERED	CORROBORATE	SCRUTINY	INEXPLICABLE	LIBERTINE
EUPHEMISMS	OBSTETRICAL	CONTINGENCY	TRAVERSED	LABRYINTH

The Great Gatsby Vocabulary

AFFECTATIONS	REDOLENT	EPIGRAM	HAUTEUR	DENIZEN
RECEPTACLES	CONVIVIAL	PNEUMATIC	CATERWAULING	EXPOSTULATION
COMMENSURATE	ADDENDA	FREE SPACE	INNUENDO	SUPERCILIOUS
SOMNAMBULATORY	RAJAH	LABRYINTH	TRAVERSED	CONTINGENCY
OBSTETRICAL	EUPHEMISMS	LIBERTINE	INEXPLICABLE	SCRUTINY

The Great Gatsby Vocabulary

LABRYINTH	EXPOSTULATION	CONVIVIAL	PREEMPTORY	OMNIBUS
AMORPHOUS	CONTINGENCY	REDOLENT	TRAVERSED	OBSTETRICAL
CORROBORATE	ROTOGRAVURE	FREE SPACE	NEBULOUS	INEXPLICABLE
DENIZEN	CARAVANSARY	RECEPTACLES	MERETRICIOUS	RAJAH
ADDENDA	RIVULETS	CORRUGATED	CONTIGUOUS	PNEUMATIC

The Great Gatsby Vocabulary

SUBTERFUGES	ERRONEOUS	UNPUNCTUAL	CATERWAULING	SCRUTINY
EXTEMPORIZING	INNUENDO	PROVINCIAL	EPIGRAM	SUPERCILIOUS
INCOHERENT	AFFECTATIONS	FREE SPACE	HAUTEUR	LIBERTINE
COMMENSURATE	PANDERED	PNEUMATIC	CONTIGUOUS	CORRUGATED
RIVULETS	ADDENDA	RAJAH	MERETRICIOUS	RECEPTACLES

The Great Gatsby Vocabulary

EXTEMPORIZING	CONTINGENCY	INNUENDO	RAJAH	AFFECTATIONS
CONTIGUOUS	ROTOGRAVURE	SCRUTINY	INCOHERENT	DENIZEN
LIBERTINE	CATERWAULING	FREE SPACE	LABRYINTH	PROVINCIAL
REDOLENT	EXPOSTULATION	PNEUMATIC	HAUTEUR	INEXPLICABLE
AMORPHOUS	PREEMPTORY	CONVIVIAL	SUBTERFUGES	EUPHEMISMS

The Great Gatsby Vocabulary

CORRUGATED	RECEPTACLES	COMMENSURATE	CARAVANSARY	CORROBORATE
OBSTETRICAL	UNPUNCTUAL	TRAVERSED	ADDENDA	RIVULETS
PANDERED	EPIGRAM	FREE SPACE	NEBULOUS	OMNIBUS
SOMNAMBULATORY	SUPERCILIOUS	EUPHEMISMS	SUBTERFUGES	CONVIVIAL
PREEMPTORY	AMORPHOUS	INEXPLICABLE	HAUTEUR	PNEUMATIC

The Great Gatsby Vocabulary

HAUTEUR	EXPOSTULATION	UNPUNCTUAL	SCRUTINY	CATERWAULING
MERETRICIOUS	RAJAH	PANDERED	REDOLENT	EUPHEMISMS
EPIGRAM	AFFECTATIONS	FREE SPACE	ERRONEOUS	SOMNAMBULATORY
INCOHERENT	LABRYINTH	CORROBORATE	NEBULOUS	OMNIBUS
EXTEMPORIZING	CARAVANSARY	OBSTETRICAL	RIVULETS	SUPERCILIOUS

The Great Gatsby Vocabulary

RECEPTACLES	CORRUGATED	LIBERTINE	CONVIVIAL	INEXPLICABLE
COMMENSURATE	PREEMPTORY	CONTIGUOUS	ROTOGRAVURE	AMORPHOUS
ADDENDA	INNUENDO	FREE SPACE	SUBTERFUGES	PNEUMATIC
DENIZEN	PROVINCIAL	SUPERCILIOUS	RIVULETS	OBSTETRICAL
CARAVANSARY	EXTEMPORIZING	OMNIBUS	NEBULOUS	CORROBORATE

The Great Gatsby Vocabulary

SUPERCILIOUS	CORRUGATED	CARAVANSARY	PROVINCIAL	LABRYINTH
OBSTETRICAL	AFFECTATIONS	INEXPLICABLE	RIVULETS	CONVIVIAL
AMORPHOUS	RECEPTACLES	FREE SPACE	DENIZEN	PANDERED
INNUENDO	EUPHEMISMS	CONTINGENCY	OMNIBUS	EXPOSTULATION
NEBULOUS	HAUTEUR	INCOHERENT	ERRONEOUS	COMMENSURATE

The Great Gatsby Vocabulary

CONTIGUOUS	MERETRICIOUS	SCRUTINY	CORROBORATE	LIBERTINE
PNEUMATIC	ADDENDA	TRAVERSED	EPIGRAM	REDOLENT
EXTEMPORIZING	CATERWAULING	FREE SPACE	UNPUNCTUAL	SOMNAMBULATORY
RAJAH	SUBTERFUGES	COMMENSURATE	ERRONEOUS	INCOHERENT
HAUTEUR	NEBULOUS	EXPOSTULATION	OMNIBUS	CONTINGENCY

www.ingramcontent.com/pod-product-compliance
Lightning Source LLC
LaVergne TN
LVHW081538060526
838200LV00048B/2130